WITH MINDS OF THEIR OWN

Eight Women Who Made A Difference:

WITH MINDS OF THEIR OWN

Boniface Hanley, O.F.M.

AVE MARIA PRESS
NOTRE DAME, INDIANA 46556

CB
RaW

———————————— About the Author ————————————

WITH MINDS OF THEIR OWN is Father Hanley's third book of biographies of heroic Christians. The others are TEN CHRISTIANS and NO STRANGERS TO VIOLENCE, NO STRANGERS TO LOVE (Ave Maria Press). Hanley, a Franciscan priest, has served in a wide variety of pastoral positions, including assignments in education and the missions. Most recently Father Hanley has served as Rector of St. Francis Church in Manhattan and pastor of St. Joseph's, a 250-year-old parish in West Milford, NJ.

From *Spiritual Doctrine of Sister Elizabeth of the Trinity*, by Marie Michel Philipon, copyright © 1940 by Newman Press, Westminster, MD. From *Elizabeth of Dijon*, by Hans Urs von Balthasar, copyright © 1956 by Pantheon, New York.

From *Jeanne Jugan* by Paul Milcent, copyright © 1980 by Darton, Longman, and Todd, London.

From *Difficult Star: The Life of Pauline Jaricot*, by Katherine Burton, copyright © 1947 by Longmans, New York.

From *Mrs. Seton: Foundress of the American Sisters of Charity*, by Joseph Dirvin, copyright © 1975 by Farrar, Straus and Giroux, New York.

From *Poustinia: Christian Spirituality of the East for Western Man*, by Catherine de Hueck Doherty, copyright © 1975 by Ave Maria Press, Notre Dame, Indiana.

From *Dorothy Day: A Biography*, by William Miller, copyright © 1982 by Harper and Row, San Francisco. From *Dorothy Day: A Radical Devotion*, by Robert Coles, copyright © 1987 by Addison-Wesley, Reading, Massachusetts.

Illustration Credits: Archives of Marquette University, Milwaukee, Wisconsin; Archives of Madonna House, Combermere, Ontario, Canada; Archives of the Sisters of Charity, Emmitsburg, Maryland; Archives of the Motherhouse of the Little Sisters of the Poor, St. Pern, France; Archives of the Carmel, Dijon, France; Archives of the National Headquarters of the Society for the Propagation of the Faith, Lyons, France; Library of Whitefriars Hall, Washington, D.C.; Courtesy of the Franciscan Friars of the Province of the Most Holy Name of Jesus, Roppongi, Tokyo, Japan.

International Standard Book Number: 0-87793-454-1

Library of Congress Catalog Card Number: 91-72117

Printed and bound in the United States of America.

Contents

Foreword 7

Dorothy Day 11

Catherine de Hueck Doherty 39

Elizabeth Ann Seton 67

Jeanne Jugan 97

Elizabeth of the Trinity 123

Pauline Jaricot 151

Teresa of Avila 179

Satoko Kitahara 205

Foreword

Throughout the centuries and around the world, women have shaped the life of the church by bringing Christ's presence to the poor in the streets, to children in the schools, and to members of religious communities searching for a deeper spirituality. From sixteenth-century Spain's Teresa of Avila to twentieth-century America's Dorothy Day, the eight women profiled in this book made this kind of a difference, often at great personal sacrifice.

These women differed from each other in many ways — nationality, social class, lifestyle, vocation, and the religions in which they were born and raised — but all were committed to living the gospel of Jesus without compromise. They were mothers, single women, and nuns. Some were born Roman Catholics, others made an adult decision to join the Catholic church. Some worked within the institutional church to deepen its spirituality through the founding and reformation of religious orders and the organization of schools and charitable organizations. Others, while maintaining a link with the institutional church, worked directly with the poor and the outcasts, fulfilling Christ's mandate to feed the hungry, give drink to the thirsty, shelter the homeless, and free the oppressed.

Often they had to overcome great obstacles and bewildering circumstances. Church authorities and even their own families and religious communities opposed their efforts at times. While some were never recognized in their lifetimes for the contributions they made, all persevered in following God's call in their lives, regardless of setbacks and seeming defeats.

The stories of these women can inspire, challenge, and encourage us. In their struggle to find meaning for their lives, they help us discover meaning for our own.

*   *   *   *   *

Catherine Doherty remembered saying of St. Francis, "I knew I would be like him some day." The Franciscans of St. Anthony's Guild, striving to be like him too, are happy to share these stories and wish the readers "peace and good" as Francis did.

We offer special acknowledgment to those who originally brought these portraits to the Guild's magazine, *The Anthonian*: To Fr. Salvator Fink, O.F.M., who selected these subjects and captured their stories in photos; Fr. Boniface Hanley, O.F.M., who wrote the texts; Fr. John Manning, O.F.M., who researched their lives. Also to Fr. Felician Foy, O.F.M., Fr. Cassian Miles, O.F.M., Rose Avato, and Janet Gianopoulos; and Mr. James Conniff of Megadot for his efforts in making this book a reality.

May the stories of these women inspire us all to make a difference.

Fr. Kevin E. Mackin, O.F.M.
Director of St. Anthony's Guild
Paterson, New Jersey

Dorothy Day

Mrs. Barrett, with the breakfast dishes done and the children off to the store, knelt to pray the rosary in the front room of her railroad flat. She had hardly begun when a tiny voice interrupted: "Mrs. Barrett, excuse me. Where's Kathryn?" The voice belonged to her daughter's playmate, Dorothy. Mrs. Barrett, remaining on her knees, turned to the little girl. "Kathryn went to the store, Dorothy. She'll be back soon."

Dorothy, a Protestant who knew little of the rosary, spun around and skipped down the long corridor and out onto the Chicago street to await her friend. Although she had left Mrs. Barrett's presence, the image of Kathryn's mother at prayer had fixed itself in her mind. "I felt a warm burst of love toward Mrs. Barrett," she wrote a half century later, "a feeling of gratitude and happiness I have never forgotten. She had God, and there was beauty and joy in her life."

The little girl, Dorothy Day, spent a lifetime seeking that God. She found him in her "long loneliness" and in the unflagging pursuit of a love that she termed "harsh and dreadful." Rarely, however, did she experience him without remembering the joy she felt, but little understood at the time, at the sight of Mrs. Barrett absorbed in prayer.

"No one wanted to go to bed, and no one ever wished to be alone." So Dorothy remembered late nights and early mornings during the winter of 1917–18 in the back room of Jimmy Wallace's Greenwich Village saloon at New York's Fourth Street and Sixth Avenue. Wallace's patrons, mostly members of the city's theater, newspaper, and artist colonies, dubbed the saloon the "Hell Hole." The Hell Hole heated up after the theaters closed, the morning newspapers were put to bed, and most respectable people were at rest.

Twenty-year-old Dorothy, a freelance writer who had previously worked for the socialist newspaper *The Call* and the Communist magazine *The Masses*, found the saloon's bohemians congenial and exciting. The tall, gawky, idealistic young woman grew friendly with playwright Eugene O'Neill. She remembered sitting at the Hell Hole bar and listening "in a sort of trance" as O'Neill, dour and dispirited, recited from memory Francis Thompson's "Hound of Heaven." The poet compared Christ's pursuit of the sinner to a hunting dog's relentless pursuit of its prey. She recalled O'Neill

As a $5-a-week reporter for the socialist *New York Call*, Dorothy crusades in word and deed; behind her sweet face was the heart of a talented muckraker.

intoning the cadences "in his grating, monotonous voice, his mouth grim, his eyes sad."

*   *   *   *   *

Dorothy won her spurs as a genuine radical shortly after the United States entered World War I. The government charged the editorial staff of *The Masses* with treason for mocking and snarling at American intervention in the conflict. The government failed to convict the writers, but the suit killed the magazine.

Shortly after the downfall of *The Masses*, Dorothy earned a thirty-day sentence in a government workhouse for demonstrating with a group of suffragettes outside the White House. U.S. Marines tore placards from the ladies' hands, crowded the protestors in police vans, and sent them off to jail. A fight erupted in the jail when male guards, suspicious that she was organizing a breakout, began to beat her. A group of her sister prisoners, kicking and biting, tried to defend her. Following the scuffle, the warden sentenced the women to six days of solitary confinement. After being released from detention and receiving pardon from President Wilson, the suffragettes succeeded in having the prison superintendent fired for brutality.

Such credentials won Dorothy the respect and admiration of the Village intelligentsia. The names of her friends and acquaintances read like a Who's Who of American radicals: John Dos Passos, Max Eastman, Mike Gold, Agnes Boulton, Floyd Dell, Hypolite Havel, Malcolm Cowley. She listened to these earnest men and women analyzing, over their drinks, formulas for peace and justice.

She admitted the conversations often confused her and failed to answer questions that had haunted her from her college days. Why, she had asked herself then, was so much done in remedying social evils instead of avoiding them in the first place? Why do we have day nurseries when we do nothing to help fathers earn enough money so mothers do not have to go to work? What compensation do we offer people for occupational diseases? What about diseases that result from not enough food for mothers and children? What about disabled workers who receive no compensation but only charity for the rest of their lives?

She could not sort out the furious currents of hate, fear, anger, greed, and passion for justice sweeping around her. "I wavered," she noted, "between my

Three of the Day children, Donald (right), Dorothy, and Sam Houston, in their Brooklyn home — all three would grow up to become outstanding journalists, but Dorothy was the radical exception to her brothers' conservative politics.

allegiance to socialism, the I.W.W. (the International Workers of the World, known as the 'Wobblies'), and anarchism."

*　　*　　*　　*　　*

Dorothy was born in Brooklyn on November 8, 1897, the third of five children. Her father, John Day, a Tennessean, married her mother, Grace Satterlee, an upstate New Yorker, at the Episcopal Church of Perry Street in Greenwich Village, not far from the Hell Hole. Journalist, racetrack writer, and member of the New York State Racing Commission, John Day was also a founder of Florida's Hialeah racetrack. The two oldest Day children, Donald and Sam Houston, became outstanding conservative journalists. Sam became managing editor of the *New York Journal American*. Dorothy shared her brothers' journalistic talents, but never their political stance.

The vicissitudes of her father's newspaper career forced him to move the family first to San Francisco, then to Chicago, and finally, in 1916, back to New York City. Dorothy left the University of Illinois to join the family when they returned to the East. Her father, however, would not allow her to live at home because she refused to return to school and insisted instead on getting a job. *The Call* hired her for five dollars a week, and she rented lodgings in a dingy East Side tenement which she said had the "smell of a grave."

*   *   *   *   *

The successful conclusion of World War I, the explosive arrival of the Roaring Twenties, and the super-heated postwar economy combined to kill the American Radical Movement. Dorothy, hanging out in Greenwich Village, continued to win prestige not for her radicalism, which interested few, but for her drinking capacity. Village habitués particularly admired her "because," writer Malcolm Cowley asserted, "she could drink them under the table." Another writer, Floyd Dell, remembered her "as an awkward and charming enthusiast, with beautiful, slanting eyes."

Just after the war and a brief nursing career in Kings County Hospital, Brooklyn, Dorothy moved in with Lionel Moise, a hard-living, hard-drinking newspaperman. Soon pregnant and fearful that Moise would dump her when he discovered it, she had an abortion. He dumped her anyhow. She attempted suicide at one point during this stormy affair.

In 1920, following the end of her affair with Moise, she married forty-two-year-old Barkeley Tobey, a New York literary promoter. Barkeley, whose eight previous marriages made him a well-practiced if not persevering groom, whisked his young bride off to London and Paris. The marriage began to come apart during the couple's stay of less than a year in Europe. Dorothy, confused, dispirited, and, by this time, world-weary, retired to the Isle of Capri to write an autobiographical novel which she wryly entitled *The Eleventh Virgin*.

The marriage broke up in 1921 on her return to the States. In Chicago, she made a futile attempt at reconciliation with Moise and re-established contact with radical friends in the I.W.W. and Communist underground.

*   *   *   *   *

In the fall of 1923, Dorothy took a job with *The Item*, a New Orleans newspaper. She began praying the rosary and attending Benediction at New Orleans Cathedral. *The Eleventh Virgin* was published in 1924 and earned her a Hollywood offer of five thousand dollars for the movie rights, whereupon she immediately returned to New York, purchased a tiny beach-front cottage on Staten Island, and settled down to write.

Each day, Dorothy left her typewriter and strode along Staten Island beaches, alone with her thoughts, her willowy body bent into the winds whipping across the bay. The salt air cleansed her heart of the scars and scabs of her previous life and, for the first time in years, she experienced inner peace. "It was a peace," she recalled, "curiously divided against itself. My very happiness made me know that there was greater happiness to be obtained from life than

Forster Batterham, here shown with Dorothy and her brother John, moved in with Dorothy on Staten Island and fathered Dorothy's daughter Tamar.

any I had ever known. I began to think, to weigh things, and it was at this time that I began consciously to pray more."

On occasion, she took the ferry to Lower Manhattan to visit her former bohemian friends, then in full cry as postwar disillusionment welled up across America. To endure the melancholy, the bohemians engaged in an endless round of partying and drinking. Dorothy recalled listening at one gathering to a conversation among writers Malcolm Cowley, Kenneth Burke, and John Dos Passos. "I could not understand one word of it," she noted.

At another reunion, she met Forster Batterham, an atheist, anarchist, and biologist. The two fell in love, and Forster moved in with her on Staten Island. He remained in the city during the week and commuted to the beach house on weekends. Eight months short of her twenty-ninth birthday, Dorothy gave birth to a girl, whom she named Tamar Teresa. Forster, long soured on the human race, did not share Dorothy's joy at the birth. He could not understand why anyone would want to bring a child into what he judged a miserable world.

Much to Forster's dismay, Dorothy, who had been praying the rosary on her walks along the beach ("Maybe I did not say it correctly, but I kept on saying it because it made me happy," she remembered) and going to Sunday Mass, announced that she wanted to have Tamar Teresa baptized in the Catholic faith. With the help of Sister Aloysia, a retired grammar school teacher who cared for orphans at nearby St. Joseph's-by-the-Sea, Dorothy began preparations. Sister Aloysia, a simple, unsophisticated woman, instructed the hard, brittle, worldly wise Dorothy three times each week. She taught the Baltimore Catechism, insisting that Dorothy memorize both questions and answers. If she stumbled, Sister rebuked her: "And you think you are intelligent? My fourth-grade pupils know more than you!"

Sister Aloysia had her own question for Dorothy: "Why do you want this child baptized while you yourself are not willing to receive the sacrament?"

Dorothy had Tamar baptized four months after her birth. Her decision enraged Forster. He despised organized religion and suspected she would soon follow their daughter to the baptismal font. "The tension between us," she wrote, "was terrible. He would not talk about the faith and would relapse into complete silence if I tried to bring up the subject."

When Dorothy was baptized in December, 1927, Forster left and never returned. "I loved Forster in every way, as a wife and as a mother, even," she wrote. "I loved his integrity and stubborn pride."

"I had no particular joy in partaking of these three sacraments, baptism, penance, and Holy Eucharist," she recalled. "One part of my mind stood at one side and kept saying, 'What are you doing? Are you sure of yourself?'"

She moved to Manhattan's Lower West Side to be able to attend daily Mass. Father Zachary, a kindly Spanish priest, guided her first shaky steps in Roman Catholicism and prepared her for confirmation. In the summer of 1929, she accepted a screenwriting job in Hollywood. After a year in California, she found the job boring and took Tamar to live in Mexico. The child fell ill, and the two returned to New York in the summer of 1930.

Dorothy hardly recognized New York. The 1929 stock market crash and subsequent worldwide economic depression had filled the once bustling streets with men, women, and children seeking scraps of food and shreds of clothing, a handout, any kind of work. Communists, exploiting widespread despair and misery, organized pressure groups throughout America. Dorothy ached to seize a leadership role, but her hard-won Catholicism, she felt, hardly encouraged her. "There was no Catholic leadership in these groups," she wrote sadly; "I felt out of it all."

The year 1929, she observed, "was the same year that Pope Pius XI said sadly to Canon Cardijn, who was organizing the young workers of Belgium, 'the workers of the world are lost to the Church.'"

Before the birth of her daughter, Dorothy had determined to raise her child in the Catholic faith. To help Tamar as well as herself, she studied the catechism and became a Roman Catholic.

Dorothy began writing a second novel and doing articles for the liberal Catholic weekly *Commonweal*. In December, 1932, *Commonweal* sent her to Washington to cover a hunger march organized under Communist auspices. The demonstration provided an opportunity for the poor to express their needs to the federal administration.

Dorothy's report revealed her deepest feelings. "On a bright sunny day, the ragged horde, triumphantly with banners flying, with lettered slogans mounted on sticks, paraded three thousand strong through the tree-flanked streets of Washington. I stood on the curb and watched them, joy and pride in the courage of this band of men and women mounting in my heart — and bitterness too that, since I was now a Catholic, with fundamental philosophical differences, I could not be out there with them."

The following day, December 8, Dorothy attended Mass in the crypt church of Washington's National Shrine of the Immaculate Conception. She offered her prayers "with tears and anguish" that the Blessed Mother would help her find a way to use what talents she possessed for "my fellow workers and for the poor."

She returned to New York. *Commonweal* editor George M. Shuster introduced her to a man who had been reading her articles and wanted to meet her. His name was Peter Maurin.

"Peter was in his mid-fifties," Dorothy observed, "and as rugged and ragged as the Washington marchers I had just left." Born into a French peasant family of twenty-three children, Maurin, a former Christian Brother and longtime scholar, had wandered the North American continent for two decades.

Peter Maurin provided the intellectual basis for the Catholic Worker Movement, while Dorothy made his poetic vision a reality in the harsh streets of New York.

Brilliant in mind and tender of heart, he had a glowing vision of humanity's future. He wrote and talked endlessly of a gospel revolution that would enable men and women to achieve a life of meaning and happiness even in this world. "Lenin," he told Dorothy, "stated 'there can be no revolution without a theory of revolution,' so I am trying to offer a theory not of a Red but of a Green Revolution!"

Maurin, who had judged from Dorothy's writings that she shared his distress with the brutal injustices of the existing social order, sought her as an ally for his Green Revolution. Dorothy, he perceived, had what he lacked — the ability to communicate his vision to the twentieth century and the hard-headed practicality to put his theories into action.

"We have to indoctrinate the people," he told her, "for the clarification of thought. We have to bring scholars and people together in round-table discussions, houses of hospitality, and agronomic universities. And we have to reach the masses through a newspaper."

In the New York offices of *The Catholic Worker*, staff members and volunteers prepare early editions of the penny-a-copy paper.

Money from a few magazine articles Dorothy had written, plus donations from two priests and a nun, added up to the fifty-seven dollars Father Joseph McSorley of New York's Paulist Press needed to publish the newspaper's first monthly issue of 2,500 copies. Dorothy and Peter decided to call the paper *The Catholic Worker* and sell it at a price anyone could afford, a penny a copy. With a few volunteers, they put together the first issue in her railroad flat at 436 East 15th Street.

On a warm, sunny day — May 1, 1933 — Dorothy and three young men sallied forth into Union Square to peddle the first issue of *The Catholic Worker*. International Communism, exploiting the collapse of the capitalist system, had been moving expertly to win the support of the unemployed. On this day, Red organizers had jammed 50,000 people into Union Square. As more than a thousand New York City police stood by, desperate workers listened to hoarse-throated orators denouncing the inherent social injustices of the American system and condemning the callous indifference of the nation's leaders to the widespread suffering of tens of thousands of these people.

Dorothy never sheltered herself from squalor and human misery. Filth and disorder, hunger and degradation only strengthened her resolve to serve Christ in the poor.

Dorothy and her troops moved among the excited crowd crying, "*Catholic Worker! Catholic Worker!* A penny a copy!" Despite vicious catcalls and curses mean enough to drive two of her volunteers to quit, she and her single assistant sold enough copies to assure her own and Peter's intuition that a market for *The Catholic Worker* really did exist.

Within three years, *The Catholic Worker* acquired a circulation of 150,000 in most countries of the English-speaking world. For almost a half century, Dorothy's column and Peter's "Easy Essays" proclaimed and explained the Green Revolution. The paper became a lively medium for Catholic intellectuals, artists, illustrators, writers, and poets seeking to apply gospel principles to modern conditions.

"When Peter talked," Dorothy recalled, "the tilt of his head, his animated expression, the warm glow in his eyes, the gestures of his hands, his shoulders, his whole body, compelled your attention." His French accent that twenty years in America had failed to erode combined with a childlike, irrepressible enthusiasm to make him a charming, irresistible salesman for his brand of Christian radicalism. His talent for persuasion was never put to better effect than when he persuaded Dorothy to take the second step of his Green Revolution, the establishment of Catholic Worker Houses of Hospitality.

By the early 1930s, thirteen million Americans had lost their jobs. Dorothy, living cheek by jowl with fellow tenement dwellers, daily witnessed the frightful suffering the economic chaos spawned. Landlords evicted people who could not pay rent, forcing whole families and their few sticks of furniture into the mean streets. People slept in alleyways, parks, abandoned buildings. Dispossessed families wandered the streets, children begged, women wept, men ground their teeth in anger.

"Peter and I saw those people standing at corners, or sitting on park benches, and we felt that something had to be done, and right away," Dorothy recalled. "We never expected to solve the nation's problems, but we thought we ought to try to do all that we could do and, we thought, if more of us tried harder and harder, well, a step would have been taken and that's what I thought the Lord wanted from us — as many steps as we could manage." At Peter's urging, she responded to the challenge with Christian hospitality.

To shelter the homeless, she rented an eight-dollar-a-month apartment near Tompkins Square, which she described as "a rat-ridden place, heatless and filthy, abandoned even by slum dwellers." Volunteers cleaned the place, and then searched for other "prime" properties to rent for evicted families. Before long, Dorothy was housing families and homeless men and women in three apartments and one storefront. On borrowed pushcarts, a tiny squad of volunteers moved the dispossessed and settled them in their new place of residence. They cooked, cleaned, and steered hapless families through the city's bureaucratic thicket until the unfortunates collected relief checks. To draw attention to the suffering of the poor, Dorothy led demonstrations, distributed literature, answered voluminous mail, and established an information office for the needy.

Dorothy began the great works of mercy that became the hallmark of the Catholic Worker Movement — works pioneered by the Wobblies and Sillon, a French labor movement. Her apartment in New York and later the House of Hospitality she established in the city and in other places across the country became newspaper offices, volunteer centers, soup kitchens, boarding houses,

From this double storefront and tenement at 115 Mott Street in New York, the Catholic Worker Movement would spread throughout the United States.

Each day, men and women from the streets were served at the Catholic Worker House of Hospitality.

Dorothy gathers with Catholic Worker House co-workers and volunteers to talk about the day's tasks and concerns.

schools, places of worship, and the center of a gospel social movement. Someone described them as "revolutionary headquarters."

Eventually, Dorothy could not afford rent for three apartments and a store-front, so she moved her homeless guests and staff volunteers under one roof. In March, 1935, she settled the group in a dilapidated four-story building at 144 West Charles Street, hard by the Hudson River. "The girls," she wrote in the April *Catholic Worker*, "with heads bound up and skirts girded about them, swished through the tomb-cold place with brooms and mops."

Within a year, the movement outgrew the Charles Street house. Dorothy then obtained, through the kindness of a benefactress, a Lower East Side ruin dating back to 1860, consisting of a tenement and two large storefronts. Located at 115 Mott Street near Chinatown, the building sheltered 150 guests and staff members. She converted the storefronts into editorial offices, a print shop, a clothing room, and dining rooms for more than eleven hundred people on the morning and evening soup lines.

"There were hundreds of them," a Catholic Worker wrote of the guests, "a silent, still crowd, with the quiet distraction of men who are missing something precious — call it the spark of ambition, interest in life, or whatever you want to call it."

Within a few years, more than thirty-three Catholic Worker Houses of Hospitality sprang up in the United States. Volunteers from every walk of life, ideological persuasion, and social standing staffed the houses. In ranks of Catholic Workers, Dorothy could count labor organizers, writers, salesgirls, scholars, widows, former members of religious orders, poets, priests, nuns, teachers, artists, factory hands, ex-cops, and businessmen. Not infrequently, guests stayed on to join the staff.

Staff members shared humble quarters, clothing, and bedding with their guests. Dorothy insisted that staff workers and guests dine together. "We know Christ in each other in the breaking of bread," she maintained. "Sitting down and eating together is the closest we ever come to each other." For as long as they chose to remain, volunteers observed the Worker lifestyle of personal poverty, service, and prayer.

Because Dorothy minimized rules and regulations, a sense of disorganization and, at times, near chaos characterized the Houses. "It would be hard to invent," reported one observer, "a more motley group of men and women. Rich and poor, young and old, notable and humble felt welcome. At meals, an eminent French philosopher or a Brazilian prelate might be seated beside a Bowery alcoholic or a mentally confused woman who thinks the drinking water is poisoned."

In 1933, Dorothy and Peter inaugurated a series of round-table discussions. At her invitation, Columbia University's Carlton J.H. Hayes, dean of American historians, led the first session.

"Not only the store where the sessions were being held was crowded," Dorothy wrote, "but so also were the kitchen and the hall. The audience was made up of unemployed men and women, plumbers, mechanics, steam fitters, sign painters, students from New York colleges, and Catholic workers in general."

A roster of premier American and European scholars led discussions in 1933 and 1934 on such weighty subjects as "Scholastic Philosophy," "Social Welfare and the State," and "Peace." After his 1934 lecture, Jacques Maritain, the French philosopher and later Princeton scholar, exclaimed: "I had found again in the Catholic Worker a little of the atmosphere of Peguy's office in Rue de la Sorbonne. So much good will, such generosity, such courage!"

Scholarly heavyweights — the likes of England's Hilaire Belloc, France's Maritain, America's Parker Moon and Harry Carman — journeyed to the storefront to share their learning with humble listeners.

Audience reaction to the stellar panel of scholars varied. Young men and women whom the Depression excluded from college found a source at which to quench their thirst for knowledge. Catholic college students, reading accounts of the proceedings in *The Catholic Worker* or participating in the lecture series,

discovered an intellectual challenge to current Catholic practice. Many, whether college graduates or not, remained with the Catholic Worker Movement and later became writers, organizers, and social activists.

Under the guidance of Dom Virgil Michel, Peter and Dorothy rooted the Catholic Worker Movement in the liturgy of the church. "Liturgy," the learned Benedictine taught, "is the basis of social action, of Christian social reconstruction and the springboard of Catholic Action. What a changed outlook the Christian would experience if he lived the implications of the Mystical Body of Christ — the core idea of the liturgy!"

*   *   *   *   *

As editor of *The Catholic Worker* and a top reporter as well, Dorothy covered major news events for the paper and her personal columns appeared monthly for almost fifty years.

After the failure in 1935 of efforts to establish on Staten Island a farm and study commune (called an agronomic university by Peter Maurin), Dorothy purchased Maryfarm, a twenty-eight-acre tract near Easton, Pennsylvania. Peter required Maryfarm workers to dedicate only four hours a day to manual labor and four hours to conversation, study, prayer. In the big farmhouse, he led discussions about employment, the role of the family, the use of leisure.

Despite their inexperience and the four-hour workday, the new farmers produced enough food to feed many visitors and transients as well as themselves. In 1937, Dorothy added forty more acres to the farm, an expansion that provided land for family homes and farms. The Maryfarm experiment inspired other Catholic Worker groups throughout the United States. Within a few years, over a dozen agronomic universities, each with its own personality and character, dotted the nation.

The tensions that wracked the Staten Island experiment soon appeared at Maryfarm. Catholic Worker commitment to gospel hospitality demanded that Workers receive all who came to them. As a result, the farms became refuges for dropouts of every kind. The stream of visitors, one commentator noted, "consumed the farms' limited resources and created an atmosphere more like a combination fresh-air camp, alcoholic recovery center, and lay retreat house than a working farm."

*   *   *   *   *

As early as 1934, Dorothy and some of her Catholic Workers joined a group of New York City department store employees on a picket line. They carried placards proclaiming, "The Pope favors unions! The Catholic Church backs a living wage!" The strikers were amazed. Some Catholic priests and lay persons wondered who gave Dorothy Day the right to speak for the pope.

Dorothy and the Catholic Workers entered with gusto into the labor struggles of the 1930s. They wrote, demonstrated, signed petitions, organized boycotts, mobilized picket lines, and secured publicity any way they could in the struggle for social justice. She refused to countenance violence and discouraged Catholic Worker efforts to provoke it. Sometimes, the Catholic Workers opposed Communists; other times, they joined them. "Why should we refuse to support a just

cause," Dorothy responded to those who accused her of Red collaboration, "just because the Communists support it?"

Dorothy's keen sense of justice, coupled with her uncompromising acceptance of evangelical poverty, chastity, and obedience, could have easily shaped her into a judgmental, finger-waving prophetess. Her enormous love for the church, however, prevented such posturing. Although aware that some bishops and priests showed little interest in the poor and, indeed, sometimes flaunted wealth in the midst of poverty, she nevertheless refused to place herself in opposition to the hierarchy.

"I have been invited many times by friends to become a warrior, to take on a cardinal, to wage war with the Church," she said. "I have always pulled back and then some people write me or tell me I am a coward. I don't know what to say to them. I did not convert with my eyes closed. I knew the Catholic Church had plenty of sin within it. How could there not be sin within a Church made up of men and women?"

"I have never wanted," she confessed, "to challenge the Church, only be part of it, obey it, and in return, receive its mercy and love, the mercy and love of Jesus."

Dorothy knew that the activities of the Catholic Worker Movement needed to be rooted in prayer.

As for living with the church's sins, to which she felt she had generously contributed, Dorothy took consolation in Father Romano Guardini's wry observation: "The Church is the cross on which Christ was crucified."

"I want to live and I want to die on that cross," she declared.

At a Westchester, New York, conference of women in the church, the seventy-two-year-old Dorothy, using the editorial "we," noted: "Yes, we have lived with the poor, with the workers, the unemployed, the sick. We have all known the long loneliness and we learned that the only solution is love, and that love comes with community."

Dorothy's home was the Roman Catholic church. Once she found it, she refused to leave it, no matter how stormy her relationships with hierarchy and laity became. Never did she challenge, even in sometimes heated battle, the right of a bishop or cardinal to exercise his authority.

* * * * *

The Spanish Civil War of 1936–1939 drew Dorothy and the Catholic Worker Movement into painful conflict with her Catholic family. When General Francisco Franco led an armed

Traveling around the country, Dorothy spoke passionately of the need for justice and peace.

revolt against the Loyalist Government in 1936, he had the sympathy and vocal support of many, if not most, American Catholics. Nervous about communist influences subverting their own nation, they hailed Franco as a champion of a Catholic crusade to rescue Spain from communism. Savage, no-quarter fighting characterized the civil war. Atrocities abounded on both sides. Loyalist hatred drove its soldiers to execute bishops, priests, and nuns in abhorrent fashion, blow up churches, shoot down Catholics coming out of church, and destroy Catholic institutions. Franco's forces, too, murdered priests and religious whom they judged to be enemies of their cause.

Generally, the secular press in the United States identified Franco and his army as fascists; the nation's Catholic press characterized the Loyalists as communists. Europe's two fascist leaders, Germany's Adolph Hitler and Italy's Benito Mussolini, sent troops and arms to support Franco; Russia's Joseph Stalin sent arms and political advisers to the Loyalists. Some Americans, convinced the Loyalists expressed Spain's democratic aspirations, formed a military unit called the Lincoln Brigade and fought, suffered, and died in brutal combat.

In an October, 1938, editorial, "On the Use of Force," Dorothy advised her readers that neither she nor the Catholic Worker family were praying for a victory for either Franco or the Loyalists. "We are praying for the Spanish people. All of them are our brothers in Christ, all of them temples of the Holy Spirit, all of them members or potential members of the Body of Christ."

She "prayed for all the world that was watching that awful war and taking sides and defending one group of murderers against another." European

The Catholic Worker Movement was a persistent voice in the peace movements of the twentieth century.

At the Catholic Worker retreat on the Hudson River, Dorothy found a place to restore her spirits with friends, quiet reflection, and writing.

intellectuals and scholars — such as the German Dominican anti-war theologian Father Francis Stratmann, French novelists Francois Mauriac and George Bernanos, and the French philosopher Jacques Maritain — made their case against the Spanish Nationalists in pages of *The Catholic Worker*. Only two American Catholic publications joined *The Catholic Worker*'s stance, *Commonweal* magazine and *The Echo*, the Buffalo diocesan paper.

Catholic Worker opposition to Franco provoked a storm of Catholic protest against the newspaper that swept through chanceries, diocesan newspaper offices and lecture halls, and echoed from rectory dining rooms to Sunday morning congregations.

Dorothy remembered that period of her life as "one of the worst times. I was always getting lectures. And priests and nuns were telling me I had gotten lost —

or worse." A few priests and nuns encouraged her. "They gave us strength," she recalled, "at a time when we needed any friendly smile and nod we could find."

*   *   *   *   *

By the early 1940s, Dorothy and Peter, as unique a pair as ever responded to the promptings of the Holy Spirit, had presented the church in the United States with a new creation. The rapid growth of the Catholic Worker Movement mirrored the concern of many young lay Catholics searching for a way in which to apply the gospel to contemporary society. Within ten years of its modest beginnings in the early 1930s, the Movement had thirty-two Houses of Hospitality in twenty-seven cities, as well as numerous smaller cells. Dorothy, the Movement's spiritual guide, traveled by bus all over the country to visit, to quell disagreements about policy, to encourage and explain the gospel character of the Movement. True to her free spirit, she allowed the various units of the Movement to function according to their own respective inspirations.

Although the Catholic Workers never enjoyed official church backing, they offered participants in the Movement an opportunity to observe evangelical poverty without the lifelong commitment required of members of religious orders. The Movement never established doctrinal requirements for its adherents, some of whom were non-Catholics. Catholicism was the bedrock of its foundation, however. Candidates enlisted for a variety of reasons, but "it was the word 'Catholic' that united us all. We would not have fought and struggled for a mere philosophical or political ideal." So stated an early Worker.

In rejecting violence during the Spanish Civil War, Dorothy had recourse to Jacques Maritain's ironic remark in a *Catholic Worker* article: "I have no desire to convert all Communists into ashes." Maritain preferred to draw people to Christ by living rather than preaching: "The preaching of the truth did not produce many conquests for Our Lord. It led him to the Cross."

While proposing Maritain's Christian pacifism as a solution to the Spanish Civil War aroused media opposition and cries of foul from many fellow Catholics, Dorothy discovered later that advocating the same policies for wartime America had far more painful consequences.

As war clouds gathered over the American horizon near the end of the 1930s, she attempted to mobilize opposition to a bill for universal conscription pending before Congress. Then, after Congress passed the measure in August, 1940, she wrote to Catholic Worker units throughout the country: "We will expect our Catholic Workers to oppose, alone and singlehandedly if necessary, the militaristic system and its propaganda." She acknowledged that the advocacy of nonviolence could make an end to the Movement. "But," she asked, "how can we sacrifice our principles or remain silent in the face of this gigantic error?"

Dorothy's letter, which her followers interpreted as an order from on high, created a split within Worker ranks. Worker units in Detroit, Cleveland, and Boston supported her absolute pacifism; units in Chicago, Seattle, and Los Angeles rejected it. In some houses, argument grew so bitter that Workers refrained from discussion.

Some of the Worker's brightest and most promising leaders reacted angrily to what they considered Dorothy's dictatorial methods. They accused her of advocating nonviolence on one hand while exercising her authority of leadership on the other to purge Workers who disagreed with her absolute pacifism. Further, they complained that she, in myopic attachment to pacifism, threatened the whole Worker Movement and all its potential. "You take the name of the whole Movement which stands for more things than conscription," the director of the Seattle House wrote her, "and tag it on this one issue, throwing out all who do not agree with you."

Dorothy denied she was imposing rigid compliance with her stand. But her protestations came too late; several houses closed immediately, others dropped the name Catholic Worker or House of Hospitality. After Pearl Harbor, only sixteen of thirty-two Worker units survived. By war's end, only ten Houses remained. *The Catholic Worker* newspaper lost 100,000 subscribers. Dorothy's advocacy of pacifism, as well as wartime conditions that brought full-time employment, combined to diminish the role of the Catholic Worker Movement in American society.

Throughout decades of bitter wrangling and demonstrations, strikes, confrontations, marches, sit-ins (at nuclear submarine bases) and climb-ins (over military base fences), Dorothy held steadfast to her belief that making peace is an essential element of the evangelical life. For her, any participation in warfare — from making weapons to serving in the military in any capacity — violated the gospel of Christ. She and the Catholic Worker Movement offered counsel

and support to citizens who withheld taxes as protest against military spending, and encouraged young men to avoid the draft.

For more than three decades, she toured the nation — speaking, writing, demonstrating, fasting, and praying for social justice and peace. Father Daniel Berrigan wrote: "What held me in thrall was an absolute stunning consistency. NO to all killing. Invasions, incursions, excusing causes, call of the blood, summons to the bloody flag, casuistic body counts, just wars, necessary wars, religious wars, needful wars, holy wars — into the fury of the murderous crosswinds went Dorothy's simple word: NO."

*   *   *   *   *

Dorothy journeyed to Rome in 1965 to attend deliberations of the Second Vatican Council on war and peace. To every bishop in the world, she gave a copy of a special edition of *The Catholic Worker* entitled "The Council and the Bomb." The council, in its *Pastoral Constitution on the Church in the Modern World*, condemned indiscriminate warfare, supported conscientious objection, linked arms expenditures with

Dorothy leads a protest against atomic weapons on the tenth anniversary of the bombing of Hiroshima.

world poverty, and allowed for evangelical nonviolence. She returned to Rome two years later to participate in the Congress of the Laity.

Dorothy's dedication to the cause of peace was acknowledged by the U.S. bishops in their 1983 pastoral letter entitled "The Challenge of Peace: God's Promise and Our Response." They called her a witness to Christian pacifism who matched her words with her deeds.

The civil rights movement and labor struggles engaged much of Dorothy's energy and concern during the 1960s and 1970s. She adapted the nonviolent civil rights strategies of Dr. Martin Luther King, Jr., to both the peace and the labor movements. For her efforts, she won the love and admiration of the poor whose interests she served. She also was shot at, shadowed by the FBI, verbally abused, and, at seventy-five years of age, imprisoned for twelve days in Fresno, California, for supporting the cause of migrant farm workers. Dorothy rather liked the Fresno jail, terming it friendlier and more charming than many others she did time in.

*   *   *   *   *

Dorothy retained her striking beauty until very late in life. Plainly dressed, peaceful of countenance, quiet in manner, her eyes bright and almost piercing, she moved placidly into old age. As long as she could breathe and walk, she worked. At the age of seventy-eight, she opened a home for bag ladies in New York and named it Maryhouse. The once brash reporter who flayed capitalist oppressors grew into a woman whose gratitude knew no bounds for the goodness

Plainly dressed, peaceful of countenance, quiet in manner, Dorothy moved placidly into old age. As long as she could breathe, she worked.

When Mother Teresa of Calcutta came to New York City, she visited Dorothy. The two women shared a common vision and dedication to serving Christ in the poor.

she experienced in everyone and everything. She even looked back to her union with Forster Batterham with gratitude in one respect. "Forster was a biologist, with a knowledge and love of nature," she said. "His ardent love of creation brought me to the Creator of all things."

Gradually, she retired more and more to her room at Maryhouse, leaving the justice and peace arenas to a new generation of Catholic Workers. A companion of many years wrote that in November, 1980, Dorothy telephoned her about the victims of Italian earthquakes. "When I explained that medicaments, food and large supplies of blankets were going in by air," the companion said, "Dorothy was relieved, saying, 'the blankets can be used as tents.'"

Dorothy died on the eve of the First Sunday of Advent, November 29, 1980, at 5:30. Her daughter, Tamar Teresa, to whom she was closely attached all her life, was with her. She was waked at Maryhouse. Thousands came to pray at her humble, pine coffin.

Two months after her death, Cardinal Terence Cooke and twenty-five priests concelebrated a memorial Mass for Dorothy at St. Patrick's Cathedral in the presence of old and new Catholic Workers and others from across the United States and Canada. In the first pew, facing the Cardinal, were Tamar Hennessy, with three of her nine children. Beside her was her father, eighty-six-year-old Forster Batterham.

Catherine
de Hueck Doherty

Red Cross nurse Catherine de Hueck wept. Her tears cut a glistening path down her broad, open face. She pressed the flat of her hands against her ears, trying to shield her mind from the angry shouts, bitter cursing, and vengeful cries exploding from the mob around her. "I promise you peace," cried the speaker haranguing the crowd. Roaring approval, listeners thrust clenched fists toward the lowering sky and pumped their arms up and down like pistons. The orator added, "I promise you bread."

He raised one hand above his head like a butcher's cleaver and held it there for a long moment. Then, fixing his fierce eyes on the crowd, he slashed it downward into the open palm of his other hand. In a hoarse whisper that reached to the crowd's ragged edges, he said, "I promise you land!"

The words cast a spell over the bruised hearts of the Russians gathered that day in 1917 in Petrograd's Smolny Square. For three years the German army had pounded these people, killing almost two million of their soldiers and maiming seven million more. Front pages of the world press featured photographs of their starving children — faces pinched, chests shrunken, bellies swollen. These people had suffered and endured beyond the reach of imagination. Now as night fell on Smolny Square, Nikolai Lenin, the messiah of a new age, promised that he would restore their dignity through the making and success of the Communist Revolution.

Several months after Lenin's harangue in Petrograd, Russia began its fateful slide into the revolutionary's grasp. The Kerensky government, the country's single feeble attempt at democracy, was overthrown in November. Czar Nicholas II, his wife, and their children were executed July 16, 1918. For a while thereafter, until 1920, the anti-Communist counterrevolutionary White Army stood against Lenin, the Red Army, and the Communist Party in the titanic struggle for control of the soul as well as the government of the Russian people.

As Catherine de Hueck listened to Lenin in Petrograd, she had no idea

that his desperate enterprise would succeed. The twenty-one-year-old nurse had spent the previous three years at the Western Front. She had survived artillery barrages, infantry attacks, airplane bombardments, near starvation, and grueling hours mending the victims of trench warfare's mindless butchery. Yet, her heart trembled as she listened to Lenin's oratory of hatred. "Lenin spellbound me," she recalled. "Only my Christian faith kept me from following him."

*   *   *   *   *

"I was born," Catherine delighted to say, "in a Pullman car." Her father, Colonel Theodore Kolychkine, and his expecting wife, Emma Thompson, had

During World War I, when Catherine was in her early twenties, she served as a Red Cross nurse in the Russian Army.

journeyed from their home in St. Petersburg (later called Petrograd and then Leningrad) to attend the great annual industrial fair at Ninji-Novgorod (now Gorki). Because thousands of visitors were crowded into the city's hotels, the Kolychkines quartered themselves in the Pullman car in which they had traveled. With little warning and a few weeks early, Catherine was born. Emma, concerned about disease, sent Catherine immediately to the local Russian Orthodox church for baptism.

Colonel Kolychkine, besides managing his farm properties, held rank in the Russian Army, served his nation's diplomatic corps, and ran a highly profitable industrial insurance business. His various pursuits required frequent travel. Whenever possible, he took his family with him. The family eventually consisted of three boys — Vsevolod (Theodore's son by a previous marriage), Serge, and Andrew — and Catherine.

French and English diplomats nicknamed the colonel "The Russian Bear." Physically awesome at six-feet-four, he had a fierce temper, a generous heart,

Catherine, with her parents, Theodore and Emma Kolychkine, in the family car during their stay in Egypt.

and a shrewd mind. He possessed an irrepressible flair for the dramatic. When he suffered severe business losses in 1906, he presented Emma with an expensive diamond pendant. "This is it for a while, Mother," he said. "We are broke."

"The Bear," as he had done before, recovered. Sometime later, he ordered Emma: "Get out your best china. Mr. John Pierpont Morgan will be dining with us tonight."

"Who," Catherine remembered her mother asking, "is Mr. John Pierpont Morgan?"

No matter where he dwelt, the Colonel practiced his charities quietly. It wasn't until after his death that the family discovered how generously he had shared his goods with the poor.

Wherever Emma established the family home, she and Catherine, twice each week, brought food, medicines, and clothing to less fortunate neighbors. When the Kolychkine women arrived at a poor person's home, Catherine scrubbed floors, windows, and doors and made beds. Emma nursed the sick. Her profound faith enabled Emma to see God's presence in every human being. "You wanted to touch God," she once told her little daughter; "touch me."

Emma raised her daughter in Russian Orthodoxy. Theodore's family belonged to the Russian Orthodox church and had some contact with Roman Catholicism during a sojourn in Poland. This blending of religious experience in the Kolychkine household enabled Catherine to develop an early appreciation of various Christian traditions.

When Catherine was six years old, her father moved the family to Turkey and then to Greece before settling down in Ramleh, a suburb of Alexandria, Egypt. Her parents enrolled her in a local school conducted by the Roman Catholic Sisters of Our Lady of Mount Sion. Catherine, who already spoke Russian, French, English, and German at home, quickly picked up Arabic from the servants and her playmates. But languages were not the only things she picked up.

She often told the story of picking up a scorpion. Innocent of the vile creature's deadly sting, she snatched it between her thumb and forefinger, and marched it home to show Emma. Emma, who immediately identified the deadly insect, fainted. Shouting for help, Catherine set the scorpion upon a glass table and stooped to help her mother. Maidservants, responding to her cries, scurried into the kitchen. Spotting the scorpion scuttling about the table top, they sent

up a hideous scream. The male Arab
cook finally arrived and dispatched the
scorpion as the maidservants struggled
to revive their mistress.

At Our Lady of Mount Sion
School, Catherine had her first sustained
contact with Roman Catholicism. The
sisters often gathered their young
charges about the statue of St. Francis
of Assisi in the school garden and told
stories about the Little Poor Man. The
stories went straight to Catherine's tender heart. "I knew I would be like him
some day," she remembered.

Colonel Kolychkine moved the
family to Paris after suffering financial
reverses in 1906. "We were poor," Catherine wrote. "It was fun." Poverty meant
down-scale living for the family. They
occupied a six-room apartment near the
Arc de Triomphe and reduced their servant staff to one. Emma and Catherine
did the shopping. "Shopping in Paris,"
Catherine recalled, "left me with beautiful memories. I loved the smell of the
foodstuffs in the stalls and the haggling."

After morning shopping, Catherine attended a private school, the Lycee
Mlle. Millard. "I learned more in one
year in Paris than I learned in ten years
anywhere else," she noted. By her

Catherine, dressed in the uniform
of Our Lady of Mount Sion
Girls' School, outside her
home in Alexandria, Egypt.

twelfth year, she could speak Greek, Italian, French, German, English, Finnish, Ukrainian, Polish, Serbian, and Bulgarian.

It took Colonel Kolychkine two years to reorganize his business affairs, whereupon he announced that the family would return to Russia. Catherine thought the news was tragic. "I loved being ruined," she recalled. "Wealth meant no more cheap flats on back streets . . . no more warm chestnuts."

The family moved into a palatial fifteen-room apartment in Petrograd. With offices in the city, the colonel acted as agent for several insurance companies, including Lloyds of London and the Equitable Society of New York. Catherine enrolled at the prestigious Princess Obolensky Academy for the nobility. Her language skills so impressed her teachers that the director of the school appointed her to teach French and German.

During these years, Catherine spent a great deal of time on the Kolychkine estate in Antrea, Finland. "I loved its old sprawling house," she remembered, "its herb room and work room, its milk cellars and pantries, its old barns, its orchards and fields."

Emma and Theodore insisted that the children share the daily chores of the estate. "I had to help the servants to serve and, in the process, to learn every household task," Catherine wrote. "I took the place of waitress, kitchen or scullery maid, baby nurse, governess, seamstress and laundress." She learned flower and vegetable gardening, animal husbandry, and beekeeping. "My mother insisted I learn all these things so I could competently manage an estate and be a gentleman-farmer's wife."

In 1908, Catherine's father rented the entire third floor of a St. Petersburg apartment for his family.

The estate had its simple pleasures. Catherine began every winter morning in an ice-cold shower, followed by a vigorous hot-towel rub. At her mother's orders, she then washed her already glowing complexion with fresh snow.

During the school term, the family remained in Petrograd. Boris de Hueck, an engineer and son of a prominent Russian industrialist and nobleman, fell under the spell of Catherine's blond hair, blue eyes, open Slavic face, and irrepressible humor. Romance blossomed, and the two were married in 1912 at St. Isaac's Cathedral in Petrograd. The marriage took place with dispensations from the Russian Orthodox church, in view of Catherine's age (15) and the couple's relationship (first cousins). They settled in Petrograd where Boris was concluding engineering studies.

When World War I erupted, Boris and Catherine enlisted in the military, he as an engineer, she as a nurse. They saw action against invading German forces, served with distinction and were cited for bravery under fire. Boris was gassed and suffered shell shock at the front. Catherine was one of many healing heroines of the war.

Following the debacle of Russian troop mutiny and military defeat, Catherine and Boris were reunited in Petrograd and were immediately sucked into the cyclone of the Communist Revolution. Drunken soldiers, thieving street urchins, hot-eyed Red zealots, the wounded, the dispossessed, and the starving lurched through the streets. Bolshevik death squads, prowling the city in search of the hated bourgeois and aristocrats, looted and murdered at will.

Red Guards vandalized the de Hueck's apartment; Catherine and Boris

Catherine accepted the privileges of wealth casually. As a young lady, she visited her Uncle Guido's luxurious summer home in Finland.

Catherine was only fifteen when she married her cousin Boris de Hueck in 1912 at St. Isaac's Cathedral in St. Petersburg.

Boris de Hueck was an engineering student and the son of a Russian industrialist and nobleman.

barely escaped with their lives. Night after freezing night, they fell asleep on the bare floor of the apartment, awaiting a knock that would signal their death. During the day, Catherine, so thin and poorly clothed that no one would think of her as an aristocrat, searched streets and garbage pails in quest of food for herself and her husband.

One day while scrounging for food, Catherine witnessed three soldiers accosting a woman clad in a Persian lamb coat. "Filthy bourgeois," cursed one soldier. He whipped out his revolver and shot the woman dead. Turning to the horrified Catherine, the murderer said, "You look poor, little girl. Take the coat." "No! No!" Catherine shouted, and ran away.

Months of near starvation left the de Huecks weak and emaciated. Desperate, they determined to escape to a cottage Boris had built as a wedding gift for

Catherine in Kiskila, Finland, close to the Russian border. They got past Red border patrols and arrived at Kiskila only to fall into a trap. Unknown to them, Kiskila's peasants had joined the Communists, looted their cottage, and occupied the property. The Reds immediately arrested the couple and sentenced them to death by starvation. They locked them in the cottage and took away all food and water, leaving only firewood so the two could warm themselves and thus prolong the agony of their death sentence.

As the dreadful days and nights wore on, tufts of Catherine's hair fell out; her teeth became loose; she fell into a coma; swelling bloated her arms and face. She promised God that, if she survived, she would give him her life. "Boris and I," she recalled, "fought over a dog bone. We were dying."

They survived, however, and were rescued by a White Finnish Army unit operating in the area. The experience of starvation haunted the irrepressible and mentally sound Catherine for years. She rarely ate much. She suffered nightmares. When she could not finish a meal, she hid what was left over.

*   *   *   *   *

Finnish and Norwegian authorities helped Boris and Catherine join Allied forces mobilizing in Murmansk to help the White Army in its attempt to overthrow Lenin's dictatorship. Boris enlisted in the British Engineers; Catherine, in the Medical Corps. Superior officers quickly recognized Catherine's linguistic talents and appointed her a translator at Allied headquarters. When the Allied forces abandoned their efforts

Catherine and Boris fled to this cottage in Finland during the Bolshevik revolution, but Red soldiers locked them in and attempted to starve them to death.

in 1919 and returned to their respective countries, her British commander arranged passage for her and her husband to Edinburgh; from there, they proceeded to London.

In London, the YMCA provided the de Huecks with a tiny attic room for an apartment in exchange for Catherine's services as a translator. The Imperial Russian Embassy employed Boris to assist in its fundraising efforts for the White Army. The British capital, suffering a severe postwar financial and spiritual depression, offered little hope of employment for Catherine. She earned a pittance sewing underwear for the Red Cross.

As Catherine returned home from work each evening, she began visiting a Roman Catholic church. "The visits strengthened and comforted me," she remembered. During these precious moments of prayer, she reflected on her and her husband's escape from death at Kiskila. She felt that God in his own good time would reveal how she could fulfill her promise to give her life to him. This faith in her future buoyed her spirits.

Although baptized Orthodox and possessing a profound love for Russian liturgy and spirituality, Catherine became a Roman Catholic in London. Her turning toward Roman Catholicism implied no rejection of her Orthodox formation, however; she simply embraced at this difficult time in her life the religion that gave her such comfort in her childhood days in Egypt and France.

Just as the two refugees nearly despaired of surviving in England, Boris, a graduate of Russia's prestigious Riga Polytechnic Institute, received an offer of a position as a landscape designer in Canada. He and Catherine jumped at the

Boris and Catherine boarded a Norwegian trawler bound for the British base at Murmansk.

opportunity. More than any other country in the world, Canada was similar to their native Russia in climate and geography.

*   *   *   *   *

Catherine and Boris arrived in Canada in March, 1921, and settled in Toronto, where their nine-pound son George was born in July at the city's general hospital.

Following his birth, Catherine became a saleslady in a large department store. She also became active in the city's sizeable Russian refugee community, and helped organize an Orthodox church to serve exiles from Russia. Canadians, curious about the Russian Revolution, began inviting her to lecture.

Despite income from their two jobs, Boris and Catherine found themselves chronically short of money. At the suggestion of her parish priest, Catherine sought job opportunities in New York City but her efforts proved fruitless. She became so discouraged that she considered hurling herself off the Brooklyn Bridge.

Eventually, she landed a job at R.H. Macy's selling perfume. She also met a number of wealthy people who invited her to dinner. She spoke so eloquently to them about her experience of war and revolution that they encouraged her to lecture under the auspices of the Chautauqua organization which, among other things, managed a bureau and program of influential speakers for appearances in the United States and Canada. The Chautauqua bureau offered her $100 a week, more than eight times the amount she was receiving from Macy's. Suddenly, she seemed to be rich.

Catherine began lecturing in 1924 in Sudbury, Canada. She spoke with such feeling about the Russian tragedy during her first talk that she burst into tears. Kindhearted listeners wept, too. Her business manager rated her performance "boffo." "If you can cry each night," he promised, "I'll raise your salary to $300 a week." When she refused to fake tears, the irrepressible agent suggested she put an onion in her handkerchief. She didn't. Even without tears, she created such demand that she was soon earning $300 a week.

Traveling by train and auto, Catherine crisscrossed Canada and the United States. She spoke in major cities, small towns, and rural areas of both nations. "Even though the constant travel wore me out," she recalled, "it gave me the chance to touch North America's grass roots."

After some time on the Chautauqua circuit, Catherine was hired in 1926 by New York City's Leigh Emmerich Lecture Bureau to recruit prominent Europeans for its circuit. She recruited so successfully and displayed such business acumen that the firm promoted her to a managerial position paying $20,000 a year. Soon thereafter, she had a Fifth Avenue apartment, a closet full of the latest fashions, a luxury automobile, and a country house at Graymoor, New York.

While Catherine's fortunes appeared to be on the rise, Boris was engaged in establishing his professional reputation in Canada. Before starting his own engineering firm, however, he took Catherine and son George to Finland in 1928 for a visit to their villa in Kiskila where his father and uncles were living. George remembered the poignant sight of his parents as they stood at a barrier on the Finnish-Russian border, looking with longing at their homeland.

During the trip, Catherine was able to visit her mother and brothers Andrew and Serge in Brussels. Her father had died earlier in Finland.

Boris' business was brought down by the financial crash of 1929; he gave it up two years later. Their marriage also failed.

On the Chatauqua lecture circuit, Catherine, dressed as a Russian noblewoman, described the horrors of Russia's Red Revolution and warned audiences that Communist atheism would destroy human rights.

"Their marriage," son George wrote, "having survived a world war, a revolution, and migration to a new country, could no longer withstand the strains of differing personalities, different religions (Boris remained Orthodox), and now economic disaster." In 1940, the marriage was annulled.

Marxist agents exploited the financial crash of 1929 by proclaiming the superiority of communism over capitalism all over the world. They found willing ears among millions of the desperate unemployed in the United States and Canada. Archbishop Neil McNeil of Toronto estimated that 28,000 members of his 96,000 largely immigrant and unemployed flock had joined the Communists. No wonder; Communists had set up centers in Toronto to feed, shelter, and indoctrinate the unemployed, dispossessed, and homeless. The Roman Catholic church in Canada, most of whose members were suffering bitterly in the Depression, did little or nothing to provide them with relief and social services.

Catherine, who had nearly succumbed to Lenin's bewitching rhetoric and had experienced Red brutality firsthand, watched with horror as Communist influence spread. For ten years, she crisscrossed the continent, warning North Americans that Communism aimed to embrace the whole world. "Its atheism," she proclaimed, "will destroy your dignity as a human person."

Her frustration mounted as her listeners, especially clergy, refused to connect Communist success with the moral collapse of Western nations. "We who fail to observe the commandments of God, especially those relating to social

Boris and Catherine pursued individual careers after arriving in Canada. Their marriage, having survived a world war, revolution, and migration to a new country, eventually collapsed under differing personalities, religions, and economic disaster.

justice, are the Communists' best friends," she warned. She saw clearly the danger of Communist ideology and influence, and cried out in frustration and pain because others could not or would not share her views.

Only Christ's gospel, she was convinced, could create the peace and justice the Marxists promised. Communist success, she believed, rested on the individual Christian's failure to observe Christ's teachings. That judgment enabled her, finally, to realize how she could fulfill the promise made while nearly starving to death at Kiskila. She determined to dedicate her life as a lay person to following the gospel of Christ without compromise.

Christ clearly stated the first condition for such commitment: "Go, sell what you have and give it to the poor. Then come, follow me." Before accepting that condition, Catherine consulted several priests. They all gave her the same counsel: "Forget it, Catherine. Your first obligation is to raise your son."

Unsatisfied with that response, she sought the advice of Archbishop Neil McNeil in 1930.

"What specifically are you planning?" he inquired.

She told him she wanted to give up all her worldly goods and live in the Toronto slums as a lay person committed to the gospel.

"You wish to become a lay apostle?"

"Yes, Bishop. By doing that I can fulfill my promise to give my life to God. I want the chance to prove the gospel is stronger than Marxism."

"Come back next year, Catherine, and we'll talk about it again."

One year later, with the archbishop's blessing, she rented a flat in downtown Toronto and began to live the gospel without compromise.

"My hands were empty," she wrote of that crucial day. "I entered a small, drab house. The smell of poverty, cabbage, and other cooking of the poor was in the air. A baby cried somewhere as I walked up a narrow stairway and entered the tiny room."

She had given away everything she did not need to provide proper housing and education for her son, George. The youth remained with her for two years in Toronto and then entered a boarding school. His experience there, as well as the other uncertainties and dislocations in his young life, proved so troublesome for George that he refused to return home; instead, he ran away to the United States. Later, he and Catherine were reconciled, and the young man continued his education in England.

Catherine went to the slums with $25 in her purse and all her possessions packed in a small, fiber suitcase. After making her first rent payment, she had precious little left for buying food. When that money ran out, she begged. Once more, the specter of starvation haunted her. Hunger she had endured before, but begging outraged her aristocratic spirit. She was seriously tempted to return to New York and seek a well-paying job.

She spent most mornings in church, attending Mass, reciting the rosary, and praying the Stations of the Cross. In the early afternoon, she moved through the slums, visiting the poor and sick, helping whomever she could with food, clothing, medicine, or whatever money she might have. Her wartime nursing experience proved invaluable.

She rented a storefront on Toronto's Portland Street and called the red-brick ruin "Friendship House."

Soon, the poor crowded into her tiny quarters. "At times," she wrote, "it seemed as if I were surrounded by desperate voices, begging hands, and tired faces streaked with tears.... I had nightmares."

George de Hueck, born in Canada in 1921, was Catherine's only child. Even while she was living among Toronto's poor, Catherine provided for his education in English and Canadian schools.

She provided three meals daily and shelter for the homeless and poor. Three women and three men volunteered to stay with her and share the work. Unsure of her responsibility to these pioneers, Catherine approached Archbishop McNeil. "What am I to do, Your Excellency? How am I to care for these people who wish to share my life of poverty?"

"Get a bigger begging basket!" he responded.

*   *   *   *   *

The year before Catherine took up residence in the slums, Archbishop Mc-Neil asked her to investigate the roots of Communist activity in Toronto. She went undercover, visited several Red cells and reported to the archbishop: "Communists are made by the hypocrisy of Christians who are Christian in name only.

In these times of depressions, the poor cry for help. Catholics are indifferent. The atheistic Communists appear, their arms laden with food and clothing . . . or send trucks filled with coal. If Catholics obeyed Christ's law of love as well as Communists obey Moscow's orders, there would be no Reds in Toronto."

The Friendship House experiment bore out her judgment. Its work so appealed to young Canadian Christians that some of them joined her in establishing Friendship Houses in Hamilton and Ottawa. Members of Toronto's academic community offered intellectual support to the experiment. Some Canadian clergy, physicians, and dentists likewise contributed their services.

Catherine, encouraged and supported by Archbishop Neil McNeil, patterned the first Friendship House in Toronto after the city's Communist centers.

The movement slowed Communist advances. Some Red cells closed; many poor families re-established themselves with the help of Friendship House. Seven young men acquainted with the work entered seminaries.

Early in the Friendship House Movement, at the suggestion and with the financial aid of Archbishop McNeil, Catherine traveled to New York for a visit with Dorothy Day, foundress of the Catholic Worker Movement. The two courageous women became fast friends and encouraged each other to persevere along the stony paths they had chosen to follow in observance of the gospel and in service to the poor.

Following the visit with Dorothy Day, Catherine's sweet taste of success turned sour. By 1937, she left Toronto under a cloud and returned to New York. A number of factors, some operating within herself, brought her down.

Despite her education, wide travel, and experience, she remained unsophisticated, even childlike. She resembled her favorite saint, Francis of Assisi, especially in her attitude toward and respect for priests. Francis, writing his last will and testament in the early years of the thirteenth century, described his

Two valiant crusaders for social justice with an uncompromising dedication to the gospel, Catherine de Hueck and Dorothy Day met in the 1930s.

personal attitude toward the clergy, some of whom were immoral and incompetent: "I desire to fear, love, and honor them and all others as my masters. I do not wish to consider sin in them because I see the Son of God in them, and they are my masters." For the same reasons as those of Francis and until her life's end, Catherine remained faithful and submissive to priests and their spiritual direction, while at the same time being critical of their shortcomings and faults.

Like Francis, she felt the need to speak out against hypocrisy and injustice. Francis, most often but not always, wrapped his reproofs in Italian tact. Catherine delivered hers with the wallop of a Russian bear. Like biblical prophets, both Francis and Catherine directed their anger against the sin, never against the sinner. She was surprised, upset, and hurt when priests or nuns reacted negatively and in a hostile manner to her reproofs for what she considered their failure to live the gospel. She was at a loss sometimes to understand North American mental processes. "I am fighting," she frequently remarked, "a whole civilization."

Many priests and nuns in Toronto supported her; others, outraged by the failure of her marriage and her bluntness, judged her to be arrogant and inimical to the church. Some even claimed she was a closet Communist. Clergy publicly expressed such feelings in question periods following her lectures. Such truculence encouraged resistance to both her message and her methods. Before long, rumors spread that she was indeed a Red agent!

Archbishop McGuigan, successor to Archbishop McNeil, supported Catherine until the drumfire of criticism reached such volume that both he and Catherine realized she must close Friendship House. "It was a terrible ordeal," she wrote. "Everything that had been built through me by God during the last six years collapsed."

She returned to New York in 1937 and landed an assignment from *Sign* magazine, a now defunct Catholic monthly, to write a series on European Catholic Action. On her trip to the Continent, she witnessed Europe stumbling into the Second World War. One of the countries she visited was Spain, already drenched in the blood of a brutal and fratricidal civil war.

The cardinal of Madrid, who had taken refuge in Salamanca far from his see city, told Catherine, according to her report, that the bishops of Spain bore a great responsibility for the savage conflict. "We paid little attention to the Pope's social encyclicals," he confessed. "I want you to know that all the parish priests in Spain who are poor have been spared by the Communists."

A lending library, here the De Porres library in
Harlem, was an important feature of Friendship House.

Catherine returned to New York from Europe in 1937. On February 14 of
the following year, she opened a Friendship House in Harlem at the suggestion of
Jesuit Father John La Farge, a civil rights pioneer. Although lecture tours across
the United States had acquainted her with racial injustice, she was unprepared
for the shock of Harlem. She could never understand how race prejudice could
infect Americans whose flag symbolized "liberty and justice for all." Still less
was she able to accept Christians practicing discrimination. With characteristic
candor, she raised the issue from lecture platform to printed page, in classrooms,
rectories, convents, and monasteries.

On one occasion, she discovered that a pastor had ejected two black women
from his church while they were praying the Stations of the Cross. She marched
the women downtown and had them relate the incident to Cardinal Spellman.

The cardinal telephoned the priest and ordered him into his office immediately to apologize to the two women.

At Fordham University, Catherine opened a lecture to the student body and faculty by telling them that for the previous three years she had attempted unsuccessfully to enroll three well-qualified black youths at Fordham. "By these rejections," she informed her audience, "your administration has told me you do not want blacks . . . and that's why I am getting off this platform right now!" Her audience, roaring in protest, insisted that she stay. She then delivered a passionate plea for interracial justice that undoubtedly influenced a later decision to revise admissions policies of the university.

Catherine concluded all of her lectures by recalling Christians asking at the Last Judgment, "Lord, when did we see you hungry, or without clothing, or sick, or in prison?" Catherine, paraphrasing Jesus' response, slowly and deliberately said: "When you were an American Catholic and I was an American Black."

Such tactics gained her few friends. Indeed, they earned her a severe beating in Savannah. Even so, she inspired enough lay followers for the establishment of Friendship Houses in Chicago, Washington, Shreveport, Louisiana, and Portland, Oregon.

"The best thing that happened to me in Harlem," Catherine often said, "was Eddie Doherty." Doherty, fifty, a nationally famous newspaper reporter, magazine writer, and screenwriter, appeared at Harlem's Friendship House to interview Catherine. "She had been there," he remembered, "nearly three years. Her hair had three shades of

Catherine often said, "The best thing that happened to me in Harlem was Eddie Doherty." The two were married in Chicago in 1943.

gold." It was love at first sight for the twice-widowed Doherty. Bishop Sheil married them in a private ceremony in Chicago in June, 1943.

Eddie, adopting the Friendship House lifestyle, settled his considerable wealth on his two sons. An alcove in the tiny apartment rented by the Dohertys served as his writing room.

*   *   *   *   *

About the time of her second marriage, stress lines, the result of differences between Catherine and her local directors, appeared in the expanding Friendship House structure. In her view, Friendship House existed to serve the poor, whatever their needs. Her directors, however, convinced that the fierce struggle for interracial justice was about to enter a new phase in postwar United States, wanted to commit the total energies of Friendship House to that effort.

Catherine's leadership style also had created tension. Trained in the European tradition, she felt that organizations functioned best when their members obeyed their legitimate authorities. Her American staff on the other hand demanded more democratic methods.

Her marriage to Eddie Doherty drew criticism from many Friendship House staffers who felt that celibacy was a powerful witness to the movement's apostolate.

Catherine left the movement in 1946. "Friendship House," she wrote, "rejected me and my ideas."

*   *   *   *   *

Eddie Doherty recalled that, at the time of their marriage in 1943, Catherine was "the loneliest person in the world." She felt that way for a variety of reasons, including the forced departure from her native Russia and the breakup of her first marriage.

Later, her experience of rejection was intensified by the antagonistic attitudes and actions of Friendship House staff members and by bitter criticism directed against her by some lay persons outside the church.

Unknown to many, she suffered a heart attack in 1947. Strong-willed as she was, she paid little attention to the advice of doctors that she should rest.

Catherine and Eddie purchased a small cottage and three acres of land in Combermere, Ontario, deep in the Canadian forests, and settled there on May 17, 1947. The retreat, about 125 miles west of Ottawa, appealed to their need for spiritual refreshment. Its silence and isolation also provided a congenial environment for the literary work by which they planned to support themselves. Reliving her farm days in Russia, Catherine planted an apple orchard, vegetable and flower gardens, and soon began raising pigs and chickens. Her agricultural and husbandry skills quickly earned the admiration and respect of Eddie and local farmers.

In the course of time, Catherine and Eddie began helping the poor people of Combermere. They collected clothing, food, and money from American and Canadian friends and delivered the proceeds to the needy. Former Friendship House volunteers and staffers began visiting their retreat, seeking counsel from their former directress. Some decided to stay. Catherine placed the property under the patronage of the Blessed Mother, calling it "Madonna House," and dedicated its growing community to the rural apostolate.

Clergy and laity, seeking periods of prayer, study, work, and rest, arrived at Madonna House in increasing numbers. With the help of benefactors, the Dohertys, over a period of about fifteen years, purchased some twelve hundred acres to accommodate the needs of the expanding community. Before long, the resident staff numbered about one hundred. They served approximately four thousand visitors annually.

Ill, disheartened, and defeated, Catherine retired with Eddie in May, 1947, to a weather-beaten cottage in Combermere, Ontario, and unwittingly provided the foundations for Madonna House.

Madonna House, a place where people could temporarily withdraw from the world for silence, prayer, and renewal, features a Russian-style shrine that symbolizes the life and death of Catherine de Hueck Doherty.

Staff members studied agriculture, arts and crafts, weaving and wool-dying, pottery, herb cultivation, the ancient Russian art of icon-painting, even cooperative marketing. Several completed studies for the priesthood. Madonna House, in response to the pleas of various bishops, eventually established twenty-two apostolic centers throughout the world.

Catherine kept a careful eye on the daily operations of Madonna House. She personally visited each new arrival, conducted classes, gave spiritual conferences every day after lunch, made the rounds of the fields, shops, and offices. She encouraged her staffers, in her Russian accent, with such exhortations as, "Move it, baby . . . let's get the show on the road!" She read voraciously and bombarded staff members with clippings from the four hundred magazines she consumed each month. She wrote no less than twenty-four books in her lifetime

— journals, poetry, spiritual treatises. Her book *Poustinia*, a summons to prayer in the silence of one's heart, received a prize from the French Academy; it has sold over 100,000 copies in the United States. Translated into several European and Oriental languages, it is about a form of Russian spirituality that has met with wide acceptance throughout the world.

Catherine carried on a voluminous correspondence. Madonna House archives contain over three hundred thousand letters she received and answered. Her letters reveal a heart filled with tender concern for her correspondents.

Clergy, religious, and laity came from all over, seeking her counsel. Despite her magnetic personality, she rejected the role of cult leader or earth mother.

"She never tied anyone to herself," a priest friend related. "She directed the person always to Christ. For example," he continued, "once, after listening to a woman relate a harrowing personal tragedy, Catherine with great compassion whispered, 'Gethsemani' and sent the woman to pray." To avoid any semblance of personality cult, she submitted all her work to appropriate church officials.

The community life of Madonna House offered Catherine the opportunity to pursue what she judged to be the only path that could lead men and women to sanity in the modern world. "The hunger for God," she wrote, "can only be satisfied by a love that is face to face, person to person. It is only in the eyes of another that we can find the Icon of Christ. We must make the other person aware we love him. If we do, he will know that God loves him. He will never hunger again."

In 1962, Catherine suffered another heart attack. "You'll be a semi-invalid the rest of your life," her doctor advised her. Once more, she told very few people about the coronary. Once more, she paid little attention to the physician's advice.

Eddie's career paralleled Catherine's at Combermere. He continued writing and lecturing. Many guests sought his spiritual direction. In 1955, because the Combermere staff had chosen a life of poverty, chastity, and obedience at Catherine's urging, she and Eddie decided to make promises of mutual chastity. Following this step, Eddie began preparing himself for ordination to the priesthood. He joined the Melkite Oriental Rite which permits a married clergy, and received holy orders in that rite in 1969. He died in 1975 at age eighty-four.

* * * * *

"It's only in the last six years," Catherine remarked to lecture audiences during the 1970s, "that I have become respectable." The indomitable woman who had been tossed out of Toronto, shelled with eggs and tomatoes in New York State, and beaten in Georgia now received one honor after another.

Beginning with the Holy See in 1960, the Canadian Government, the French Academy, three United States and two Canadian institutions of higher learning all conferred honors upon her. In 1976, after accepting membership in the Order of Canada, the country's highest honor, Catherine, who had drunk deep of rejection's bitter cup, stood silent for a long moment. "It's nice," she then said, "to be accepted. It means a lot."

* * * * *

From the time of her girlhood sojourn in Egypt, Catherine had chosen St. Francis of Assisi as her model. As her physical powers became weaker with the passage of years, she grew more and more like the gentle Poverello who spent his last two years on Italy's Mount Alverna in close union with the sufferings of Jesus.

At Madonna House in the Canadian forest, she saw God everywhere. A Madonna House priest recalled sitting in a small office with her, his back to the closed door. Without knocking, someone opened the door. "Catherine's face," the priest remembered, "shone with such radiance that I thought Christ had come to

Although limited by physical illness, Catherine continued to be a spiritual force in the Madonna House apostolate.

take her home. It wasn't Christ at all," however. "It was one of the Madonna House workers."

Like Francis, she felt a kinship with all of creation. Returning home from a trip on one occasion, she discovered to her deep distress that workmen had cut down a rotting maple tree next to her little cottage. "I wanted, at least," she complained, "to say goodbye to an old friend."

Soon after serious illness hobbled her in August, 1981, Catherine wrote: "It never occurs to us that tomorrow, or the day after, our steps will falter, that we will be too weak to do this or that. Yet, no one can stop me from entering the landscape of God." The Russian dynamo, the fearless champion, the rugged battler for human rights spent her days wrapped in silence with Jesus crucified. "So here we are together," she wrote, "He and I. He is bound, too. Bound with nails. Perhaps he binds me to keep me close to him." Then in one final stirring profession of faith she concluded: "Little do they know that, when they bind me, a window is always left open, and I go and lose myself in God."

She died December 14, 1985. Her final legacy, Madonna House, flourishes to this day.

Catherine's simple grave marker in the Madonna House cemetary sums up her life's faithfulness to a gospel without compromise: "She loved the poor."

A few years before she died, Catherine wrote a paragraph that summed up her life and times.

"This is the era of the Spirit. Vatican II shook us all up as powerful winds are wont to do. Mighty trees fell. As they fell, they tore up a lot of underbrush that had begun to grow over the paths of the Lord. Yet, let us be full of hope. Although shaken up, we truly have been thrown into the arms of hope — wondrous, soul-healing, joyous hope."

Elizabeth Ann Seton

New Yorkers were enjoying a sparkling fall day, October 2, 1803. Huge white clouds, like great gondolas of light, sailed majestically across Manhattan's porcelain-blue skies. Offshore, forest and marshlands bursting into their autumnal colors framed the city's lower Bay with a rich riot of color...deep reds, scarlets, greens, russets, browns, yellows, golds, purples. Fresh breezes danced over the Bay and the waters responded with ripples of delight.

In the harbor, longboats were gently coaxing a large sailing vessel, *The Shepherdess*, Captain O'Brien commanding, into the outgoing tide. Skillfully the crew brought the brigantine's madly flapping sails under control until, filled with the autumn breezes, they swelled roundly and proudly in the afternoon sun. Little by little, the trim vessel, commanded now by the harbor pilot, picked up speed. Her destination was Leghorn, Italy. Passengers and crew knew the voyage would be long, some seven weeks, and probably perilous. Pirates still roamed the Atlantic, and the sea was full of war and violence.

A married couple, Mr. and Mrs. William Seton, with their eldest daughter, Anna Maria, eight, stood on the deck of *The Shepherdess*, waving farewell to their four younger children and a little knot of relatives on shore. William Seton broke into tears, and the tuberculosis wracking his body caused him a fit of

This sketch shows New York harbor in 1772, two years before Elizabeth Seton was born.

uncontrollable coughing. Although he was taking this voyage as a remedy for his illness, Will Seton knew this could be his last earthly sight of his little ones. His wife, Elizabeth, bowed over by grief, could no longer wave her little handkerchief to her children. She later recalled that she did not believe her heart could know so much pain and not break.

The voyage of *The Shepherdess* had begun. For Elizabeth Ann Seton, daughter of the eminent New York physician Dr. Richard Bayley, it was to be a journey into destiny, a destiny beyond the imagination of Mrs. Seton or any other person on board *The Shepherdess* that day.

*   *   *   *   *

Richard Bayley was an excellent doctor, and he knew it. Member of a prominent Colonial family, Richard began medical studies in New York City in 1764 under Dr. John Charlton, a famous society physician. Before finishing his studies, four years later, Bayley not only absorbed Dr. Charlton's skills, but also married the physician's sister Catherine in 1767.

The new bride soon learned that she took second place to her husband's profession. The first year of their marriage had not yet ended when Dr. Bayley left Catherine in New York to continue surgery studies in London. While her husband was in England, Catherine bore their first child and named her Mary Magdalen. A year after Mary's birth, Dr. Bayley returned to New York and continued a career that would establish him as a great American medical pioneer. Catherine bore a second daughter on August 28, 1774. The Bayleys, Episcopalians, christened her Elizabeth Ann. Some months after the new baby's arrival, her father once more embarked for further studies in London. But the American Revolution broke out, and young Dr. Bayley, a Tory, returned to America as a medical officer in the British army. Catherine's hopes that her husband would be near the family during the Revolution's dangerous days were short-lived. Superiors assigned Richard to the British military hospital in Newport, Rhode Island.

In March, 1777, Bayley received word that his wife, pregnant with their third child, was very ill. Resigning his commission, Dr. Bayley rushed to Catherine's bedside in Newtown, Long Island, a village just outside of New York City. There, with Elizabeth and Mary, Catherine awaited the arrival of the new baby and the summons of death. The new child survived and was called after her mother, Catherine. Mrs. Bayley, who died soon after Catherine's birth, had been married to her husband and his profession for eight hard years.

The sidewalks of New York had not yet been built when Elizabeth walked through the streets to school and to local shops.

*   *   *   *   *

In June, 1778, Dr. Bayley married Charlotte Amelia Barclay, daughter of Andrew and Helena Roosevelt Barclay. The following October, baby Catherine Bayley, born in her mother's suffering and pain, died. Her four-year-old sister, Elizabeth Ann, remembered those sorrowful days a quarter of a century later: "Sitting alone on the step of the door," she wrote, "looking at the clouds while my little sister Catherine, two years old, lay in her coffin, they asked me, Did I not cry when little Kitty was dead? No, because Kitty is gone up to heaven. I wish I could go, too, with Mama."

Strange and melancholy thoughts for a four-year-old. But Elizabeth Ann's early life had its strange and melancholy hours. Endowed with her father's deep intelligence, as well as a sensitive personality and strong will, Elizabeth Ann was a most complex little girl. Deprived of her mother's and baby sister's love, and forced to live with a stepmother who disliked her, Elizabeth turned wistfully to her busy father, whom she adored. Although he loved her more than any of his other children, Dr. Bayley would not let his little Betty interfere in his medical career, any more than he would her mother.

Dr. Bayley did ensure his girls' proper education. He enrolled Elizabeth in an excellent New York City private school, under the direction of "Mama Pompelion." Here Betty learned French and music and received the rudiments of education. If little Betty Bayley, peering out the school window, saw her father making his rounds, she would slip quietly from the classroom to run and kiss him. A lonely child, she needed to reassure herself constantly of her father's love.

*   *   *   *   *

Charlotte Barclay bore Dr. Bayley seven children. But Mary and Elizabeth never felt at home in this household. To ease the friction between his second wife and his daughters, Dr. Bayley sent Mary and Elizabeth to his brother William's home in New Rochelle, New York. Kindly Uncle William's pleasant estate bordered Long Island Sound. Elizabeth Ann discovered nature's beauty and riches in solitary rambles along the shores of the sound. To compensate for her own father's neglect, eight-year-old Elizabeth began to search for her heavenly Father in nature. "Every little leaf and flower or animal, insect, shades of clouds, or waving trees," she later wrote, "were objects of vacant, unconnected thoughts of God in heaven." She searched, not only for God, but for her mother and her baby sister.

"I delighted to gaze at [the clouds], always with the look for my mother and little Kitty in heaven," she recalled.

In her loneliness, Elizabeth discovered resources of strength and, surprisingly, joy. She wandered for hours along the shore, singing into the salty winds, and at times into the night, her eyes full of the stars and her ears soothed by the rustling of the trees.

"I took pleasure in everything, coarse, rough, smooth, or easy — I was always gay, [with] joy in God, that he was my Father."

Her contacts with her earthly father were, at best, irregular. During Elizabeth's fifteenth year he was again in England. Richard couldn't find time during his two years' absence to write home. "My father away," Elizabeth noted in her memoirs, "perhaps dead."

One morning during her father's English sojourn, Betty became intensely aware of God's presence. "I was in the woods alone," she remembered; "the sun was warm. The numberless sounds of spring melody and joy — the sweet clovers and wild flowers I had got by the way, and a heart as innocent as human heart could be, filled even with enthusiastic love of God and admiration of his works. . . .

"God was my Father, my all. I prayed, sang hymns, cried, laughed, talking to myself of how far he could place me above all sorrow. And I laid still, to enjoy the heavenly peace that came over my

Elizabeth discovered God's consoling presence in the glory of creation as she wandered for hours along the shores of New York Sound.

my soul; and I am sure, in the two hours so enjoyed, I grew ten years in the spiritual life."

Gradually, but inevitably, the heavenly Father was shaping and deepening her heart to fill it with his love.

Elizabeth's passage through adolescence was marked by extremes of joy and sadness. At eighteen, she wrote, "I was very miserable. God was too good to condemn so poor a creature made of dust." Cryptically she mentions laudanum, a powerful drug, and notes she has "excessive joy not to have done the horrid deed." What did she mean by this notation? Did she contemplate suicide? We simply do not know.

*   *   *   *   *

The mercurial young Elizabeth reflected her mother's French ancestry in both her personality and her great natural charm and beauty. A bit below medium height, she was slight, graceful, and well proportioned. Contemporaries speak of her dark and lustrous eyes, dark complexion, and fine features. Educated beyond most women of her day, Elizabeth's mind bore the Bayley genius. She spoke fluent French, could write poetry, play the piano, and possessed a keen and inquisitive intelligence. Her Gallic vivacity bubbled over into a love for the theater, dancing, and New York's lively postrevolutionary society. The city was then the nation's capital, and Miss Bayley, an accomplished horsewoman, undoubtedly met President Washington on Manhattan's riding paths.

And now Elizabeth Ann, no stranger to loneliness, was to meet a man who would fill her heart with his affection and love. Scion of a famous New York financial family, William Seton moved easily among the city's first families. Among his friends and acquaintances he numbered the Jays, the Livingstons, the Hamiltons, the Bayleys, the Roosevelts, the Vanderbilts, and other distinguished families.

William Seton, Sr., had carefully prepared his son to assume control of the family's vast international commercial interests. Young William had studied in England and traveled about Europe's financial centers to meet many of his father's business associates.

Sometime in 1791, the tall, cultured and favored young William met Elizabeth Bayley. A gay and joyous courtship began. Elizabeth blossomed in the warmth of William's attentions.

On January 25, 1794, the Right Reverend Samuel Provoost, rector of Trinity Church and first bishop of the Protestant Episcopal Diocese of New York, married William Magee Seton and Elizabeth Ann Bayley. Betty was nineteen and Will was twenty-five and the future was bright.

The newlyweds established their home at 27 Wall Street — in those days a very posh address indeed. The Alexander Hamiltons were neighbors, and Betty bought her furniture from Duncan Phyfe's nearby shop. In May, 1795, Betty gave birth to her first child, Anna Maria. The next year, in November, Betty presented William Seton with their first son, William III. With the new year of 1798 Betty learned she was carrying another child. She and William were delighted.

But before she bore this baby, disaster struck the Setons. William's father, founder of the family fortune, unexpectedly died as a result of a fall. He was fifty-two. For William, Jr., the blow was devastating and irreparable. It would not take long for everyone to know what William himself probably sensed. He simply did not have his father's business talent. Also, as eldest son, he accepted the responsibility of raising his brothers and sisters. Betty Seton suddenly had nine children.

She almost died during the birth of her third child, Richard, and her father had to employ mouth-to-mouth resuscitation to get the little baby's lungs working.

The summer of Richard's birth, a wave of yellow fever struck New York. Will Seton, who had inherited a tendency to tuberculosis from his Seton

Sometime in 1791, William Magee Seton, son of a prominent New York financial family, met Elizabeth Bayley, and a joyous courtship began.

ancestors, nevertheless continued working each day, struggling to keep control of his father's business interests and to support the large family now given into his care. Sickness plagued the Seton household all summer and winter.

Dr. Bayley worked ceaselessly during the plague. Whatever his faults and shortcomings, Dr. Bayley never neglected any sick person, rich or poor. It was probably his relentless dedication to his profession that caused his second marriage to break up in the spring of 1799. After leaving his wife and children, Bayley, New York City's Chief Health Officer, began construction of health stations for immigrant quarantine and a personal residence near Tompkinsville, Staten Island.

The following year, Dr. Bayley invited William and Elizabeth and their large family to spend the summers at Staten Island. Elizabeth, who had just given birth to her fourth child, Catherine Josephine, in June, 1800, was delighted. The home, boasting an upper balcony commanding "a view fifty miles beyond Sandy Hook," rang with children's shouts, cries, and laughter. Elizabeth, a pianist, and Will, a violinist, filled the summer nights with sweet music.

William and Elizabeth Seton built their first home on Wall Street, then the city's prime residential area.

* * * * *

International unrest, piracy on the high seas, and general disorder throughout the international financial community, combined to shake the foundations of the Setons' European and American business enterprises. William could neither master nor control the events and pressures closing in upon him. By now afflicted with chronic tuberculosis, Will feared for his family's future. At times the young father was frantic with worry and at other times was sunk in deep apathy. By Christmas, 1800, two and a half years after his father died, young Seton lost control of the business altogether and declared bankruptcy. To pay his creditors, he and Elizabeth sold the Wall Street home and watched as claimants possessed its beautiful furnishings one by one.

Far from panicking, Elizabeth accepted the crisis with amazing calm. From her new and more modest home in New York's Battery section, she wrote her friend Julia Scott: "Seton is quietly writing by my side in as perfect health as he has ever enjoyed — my chicks quiet in bed and my father smiling over a list of books he has just made of those he chooses to retain as one of our creditors.

Financial disaster following the death of William's father meant that the Setons had to move to a new home, this one on State Street, facing Battery Park.

For myself, I think the greatest happiness of this life is to be released from the cares and formalities of what is called the world. My world is my family, and all the change to me will be that I can devote myself unmolested to my treasure."

Elizabeth returned to Staten Island for the summer of 1801. Will, still struggling amid the ruins of his business in the city, sailed over to spend weekends with the family. Elizabeth, expressing the sentiments of generations of summer weekend wives, wrote: "This is a strange way of living — meeting but once a week — and then Will weary and out of spirits."

During that summer, Dr. Bayley worked ceaselessly at the quarantine station. Vessels arrived almost daily, disgorging hundreds of ill and often dying immigrants. Little children particularly suffered from the unhealthy conditions aboard immigrant ships. In August, Dr. Bayley contracted an infectious disease from his immigrant patients, and within a week died. He was fifty-seven.

Elizabeth's summer had come to an end. As she did when a child, Elizabeth turned to her heavenly Father as the only unchanging Presence she knew. On Ascension Day, 1802, she wrote: "Oh, that my soul might go up with my blessed Lord — that it might be where he is also. Thy will be done. My time is in thy hands, but O my Savior, while the pilgrimage of this life must still go on to fulfill thy gracious purpose, let the spirit of my mind follow thee to thy mansions of glory. To thee alone it belongs. Receive it in mercy, perfect it in truth, and preserve it unspotted from the world." That same summer, 1802, Rebecca Seton, the fifth and last child of Will and Elizabeth Seton, was born.

*   *   *   *   *

Because William's health continued to worsen, Elizabeth planned to take him to Italy at his physician's suggestion. The sea voyage and the change of air offered one slim chance to stave off Will's rapidly approaching death. Thus the two, with eight-year-old Anna, sailed from New York on *The Shepherdess* on October 2, 1803. Despite threats of war and piracy, the sea journey passed uneventfully. *The Shepherdess* sailed into Leghorn's harbor in late November. Dockside, an Italian band played "Hail Columbia," and the Setons joyfully anticipated stepping onto dry and steady ground. But events took a strange and tragic twist. Italian health authorities, aware of New York's yellow fever epidemic, forbade the disembarking of *The Shepherdess'* passengers and crew. Instead, they

This rare sketch of the ship *The Shepherdess*, on which the Setons sailed to Italy for William's health, was found in the New York Historical Society's archives.

detained them for a month in the Leghorn quarantine. The quarantine station, called "the lazaretto," was a great stone edifice located on a canal bank several miles from Leghorn's harbor. Damp and sometimes bitter cold winds blew through the prisonlike building. William, forced to bed, constantly coughed, and hemorrhaged.

Elizabeth, angered at this callous treatment, wrote: "To keep a person who comes to your country for his life, thirty days shut up between damp walls, smoke and wind from all corners blowing even the curtain that surrounds his bed, and his bones almost through and now the shadow of death, trembling if he only stands a few minutes. He is to go to Pisa for his health. These days his prospects are far from Pisa."

Italian authorities, satisfied that no yellow fever lurked among *The Shepherdess'* people, finally released them on December 18. Elizabeth hurried William and Anna to Pisa, where Seton business associates had put a villa at their disposal. There, in a strange home, in a foreign land, William Seton died, two days after Christmas, 1803. "His soul was released," wrote his wife, "and mine." Accompanied by a group of English and Americans, she buried William Seton in Leghorn's English burial ground the next morning.

The Filicchi family, prominent Italian financiers, had been Seton business associates and close friends for many years. As a young man, William Seton had studied banking with the Filicchi brothers, Filippo and Antonio, in Leghorn. The Filicchi firm had enormous banking interests in America, and the brothers moved easily in the highest American financial and social circles. Filippo Filicchi had married Mary Cowper of Boston; and General George Washington, impressed by his knowledge and integrity, appointed him United States Consul General in Leghorn.

The Filicchi family's villa in Leghorn, Italy, offered Elizabeth a much-needed resting place after William's tragic death in Pisa.

The Filicchis, Antonio and Amabilia, shared their faith as well as their hospitality with Elizabeth and aroused her interest in Roman Catholicism.

The Filicchis did all they could to ease Elizabeth's sad plight after William's death. Again and again Elizabeth's attempts to return to the United States were frustrated.

It was four long months before Elizabeth could return home. During these days, Elizabeth visited various chapels and churches. The evident devotion of the Italians who knelt with such prayerful spirit during Mass deeply moved the Episcopalian Elizabeth Seton. Roman Catholics, she heard, believed that Christ was truly and really present in the eucharist. The air of deep mystery and peace surrounding the worshiping people was rooted in this presence. She wrote her sister-in-law, Rebecca Seton: "How happy we would be if we believed what these dear souls believe: that they possess God in the Sacrament and that he remains in their churches and is carried to them when they are sick!" For the little girl who had sought God in the clouds above New Rochelle, this belief was too good to be true.

Elizabeth questioned the Filicchis regarding Catholic beliefs. Although they frankly expressed their wish to see Betty embrace Roman Catholicism, they knew that was a decision only she could make. "Pray and see," Antonio advised. Elizabeth, now uneasy, prayed for peace of mind. This poem became her favorite prayer:

> If I am right, thy grace impart,
> Still in the right to stay:
> If I am wrong, teach,
>   oh teach my heart
> To find the better way.

In April, 1804, Elizabeth embarked for home. Because ladies did not travel alone, Antonio Filicchi accompanied her to America. He had business in the United States. An entry in her journal notes very clearly that the two of them were attracted to each other spiritually and physically. For a time they suffered grievous temptation. Both of them prayed simply and humbly for deliverance, and God granted it to them. During the fifty-six days on the seas, Antonio continued to instruct and advise Elizabeth regarding the Roman Catholic religion.

*   *   *   *   *

In June, 1804, Elizabeth returned to her native New York and her relieved friends and family. Her heart swelled as she embraced her children and saw that little Rebecca was well. It was so good to be home.

Elizabeth, however, was not to shake off her Italian experience easily. Contact with Catholicism had changed forever the pattern of her life. Soon after returning, she spoke to her former spiritual director, the popular Episcopalian minister, Reverend John Henry Hobart. Since the dreadful winter after she had lost her home on Wall Street, the Reverend Hobart, curate at New York's Trinity Church, had guided Elizabeth as she built a firm and solid spiritual foundation. Skillfully he steered her through her flirtation with Rousseau's romantic and emotional doctrines and helped her express her Christianity through practical works of charity. Before leaving for Italy, Hobart had warned her of "the splendid and sumptuous worship of Italy." And now, when she advised her mentor of

Elizabeth, an Episcopalian, had worshipped in New York's Trinity Church, with the Reverend Henry John Hobart (inset) as her spiritual director. When she returned from Italy, Hobart cautioned her against her new-found attraction to the Filicchis' religion.

her attraction to Catholicism, he was shocked. A brilliant and persuasive man, the Reverend Hobart marshaled every argument possible against Mrs. Seton's accepting Catholicism.

If Hobart did not dissuade her, he did unsettle her mind. Antonio Filicchi, still in the States, provided literature for her to counter Hobart's arguments. Elizabeth was trapped in a maze of internal torture and self-doubt.

Along with theological considerations, Elizabeth had to face the financial implications of a change of religion. There was a certain clubbiness among New York's first families, and Elizabeth could rightly assume they would discreetly come to her aid as she struggled to raise her fatherless family of five. Indeed, soon after her return, friends had helped her re-establish herself in a small neat house just outside the city. Elizabeth knew, too, that a change of religion would alter her relationship with many who now willingly supported her and her family. To become a Catholic was to join an immigrant religion, whose congregation was composed of the city's lowest elements. Furthermore, Elizabeth Seton's forebears, both Bayleys and Charltons, were deeply

Praying in St. Paul's Episcopal Church, Elizabeth found herself turning toward the Catholic church in the next street and praying to the eucharistic presence there as she wrestled with her decision to embrace Roman Catholicism.

rooted in the French Huguenot tradition. American Huguenots bitterly recalled their unhappy persecution at the hands of France's Catholic church. "Our Betty," her Huguenot relatives lamented, "is thinking of embracing the religion that persecuted our forefathers."

For months Elizabeth was torn between the Protestantism she loved and the Catholicism she did not yet fully understand. She prayed for light, and light did not come. She wrote to a friend about her visit to St. Paul's Episcopal Church, where she went to seek peace: "I got in a side pew which turned my face toward the Catholic Church in the next street and found myself twenty times speaking to the Blessed Sacrament there, instead of looking at the naked altar where I was, or minding the routine of prayers. Tears plenty and sighs. . . silent and deep. . . all turning to the one only desire, to see the way most pleasing to my God — whichever that way is!" At one moment she was ready to rush into Catholicism and then the next to draw fearfully back. Clouds of doubt darkened her soul, and she could only cry out for mercy. In a life often scarred with loneliness, she had never felt more alone.

But the darkness lifted suddenly in the winter of 1805, and the moment of decision came suddenly and quickly. She wrote to a friend: "I will go peacefully and firmly to the Catholic Church. I am between laughing all the while, but it is on God himself that I pin my faith. It is his affair now."

Father Matthew O'Brien and Antonio Filicchi witnessed her profession of faith at St. Peter's Church, Barclay Street, March 14, 1805. With her doubts resolved, her natural gaiety returned. She wrote, after her profession of faith, "I came up light of heart and cool of head the first time in these many long months." Father O'Brien did not rebaptize her a Catholic, accepting the Episcopalian baptism. He heard her first confession and then, on March 25, Elizabeth Seton, for the first time, received the eucharist her heart so longed for. She wrote: "God is mine and I am his! Now, let all go its rounds — I have received him." She was amazed at her reaction and she wondered, ". . . instead of the humble tender welcome I had expected to give him, it was but a triumph of joy and gladness that the deliverer was come and my defense and shield and strength and salvation made mine for this world and the next."

News of Elizabeth's conversion provoked reactions that varied from shock to pity. Some thought that Antonio Filicchi had taken advantage of the bewildered widow. "Poor, deluded Mrs. Seton," they fretted. Patronized and pitied, Elizabeth complained, "It really seems that in the estimation of my family and friends, I am a child not to be trusted with his daily bread, lest I should waste it."

Most distressing was her farewell to her beloved Reverend John Henry Hobart. His last onslaught against her conversion failed. He forgot, as so many others did, that Elizabeth bore the hot Bayley blood within her. It was for her a painful conversation. "But my faith," she dryly remarked, "was more strengthened and decided than if it had not been attacked."

Some took Elizabeth's conversion as an excuse to cut whatever financial assistance they were providing. Others, however, stood loyally beside her. Yet, Elizabeth, proud and independent, could not depend on charity alone, no matter how generously it was offered.

Like a hardy flower growing through concrete, Elizabeth's French love of fine manners survived her poverty. Typically, she thanks a friend for a gift of one hundred dollars and adds: ". . . on the head of it, Anna [her daughter] will attend an excellent dancing master at Mrs. Farquhars . . ., not for the steps but to obtain a little polish."

She made four separate attempts to establish schools in the city, hoping to raise income from her teaching and boarding students to provide a decent livelihood for her family. All attempts failed. The very people who would send their children to her school wanted nothing to do with her Catholicism. Her family suggested she try something else. "Some proposals have been made me," Elizabeth wrote with some irritation, "of keeping a tea store or china shop or small school for little children too young, I suppose, to be taught the Hail Mary. In short . . . they do not know what to do with me, but God does and when his blessed time is come, we shall know." God's blessed time was about to come.

*   *   *   *   *

Despite repeated failures, Elizabeth Seton could still dream. She hoped one day, when her obligations to her children were fulfilled, to become a religious sister and teach. Over a cup of coffee in St. Peter's rectory, New York City, one November morning in 1806, she met Father William Valentine DuBourg, president of St. Mary's College, Baltimore. DuBourg had heard in Baltimore of Elizabeth's conversion and subsequent trials. When she confided to him her dreams of teaching and entering religious life, the Baltimore priest immediately went into action. Convinced that Elizabeth would find many pupils among Baltimore's large Catholic population, he invited her to that city. Quickly he located a suitable house on Paca Street, next to St. Mary's College. "It is a mansion," Elizabeth marveled, "in the French style."

DuBourg, a man of vision as well as action, helped Elizabeth establish the particular character of her new school. He wrote: "There are in the country...mixed schools, in which ornamental accomplishments are the only object of education; we have none, that I know, where this acquisition is connected with and made subservient to pious [i.e. religious] instruction, and such a one you certainly wish yours to be." From the very beginning, Elizabeth Seton shared DuBourg's philosophy of education, which held that all the other subjects were to be subservient to religious education.

In June, 1808, Elizabeth arrived in Baltimore with her three daughters to open her school. Her two sons, Richard and William, who had been boarding for the past two years at the new Jesuit college in Georgetown, Washington, D.C., soon moved to St. Mary's College in Baltimore. Elizabeth realized part of her dream when she began at Paca Street. The other part, becoming a religious, was still in the planning stage. There is no doubt, however, that Father DuBourg felt he could establish a religious community at Paca Street, with Elizabeth at its helm. What was she to do with her three daughters? Elizabeth herself did not know. Although she saw that her first obligation was to her family, and she planned to fulfill it, she had confidence that God would show the way.

Reverend William Valentine DuBourg, president of St. Mary's College, Baltimore, shared Elizabeth's dream of establishing a school in which all teaching would be infused by religious faith.

With the encouragement of the American hierarchy, and the guidance of her priest-directors, Elizabeth began to plan. In October, 1808, only four months after Elizabeth came to Baltimore, two young Philadelphia ladies, Cecilia O'Conway and Maria Murphy, sought permission to join the new religious "community." On December 7, 1808, Cecilia O'Conway became the first religious daughter of Elizabeth Seton, joining her at Paca Street.

*   *   *   *   *

During the fall and winter of 1808–1809, Elizabeth felt strong and equal to the tasks of establishing the school and shaping her new religious community. No small credit for this belonged to her new spiritual director, Father Pierre Babade. Very much like Elizabeth in character and temperament, the priest filled her with confidence and zeal. Babade, perceiving Elizabeth's deep need for the Lord's presence, went counter to the day's spirituality and permitted her to receive the eucharist daily. The eucharist was her rock and source of strength. "Oh," she advised, "when we are sick of ourselves, weakened on all sides, discouraged with repeated relapses, wearied with sin and sorrow, we gently, sweetly lay the whole account at his feet! Merciful Savior, can there be any comparison to this blessedness?"

Father Babade had his own dream. He had dreamed for fifteen years of

Elizabeth Seton moved with her three daughters to Baltimore, where she opened a school on Paca Street.

These simple furnishings have been preserved in the small stone farmhouse in Emmitsburg, Maryland, which was the first home for the American Sisters of Charity.

establishing in America the Daughters of Charity, the famous French religious congregation. He knew that women could make a profound and solid contribution to the infant American church. He felt he now knew the woman who could successfully pioneer the effort, Elizabeth Seton. The only requirement now lacking was money, and that came from a most unexpected source.

Samuel Sutherland Cooper, a convert to Catholicism and former sea captain, studying for the priesthood at St. Mary's, shared Father Babade's vision of religious women contributing to the growth of the American Catholic church. Cooper offered ten thousand dollars to establish a pioneer foundation for women religious. He insisted, however, that the new center be established on an old farm in Emmitsburg, some fifty miles from Baltimore. After much hesitation, John Carroll, now archbishop of Baltimore, approved the site at Emmitsburg and Elizabeth's appointment as the new community's Mother Superior.

On March 25, 1809, Elizabeth Seton pronounced her vows of poverty, chastity, and obedience, for one year. From this day on, Elizabeth became known as Mother Seton. By June, her little group had grown to four, and these new recruits, with Elizabeth at their head, donned, for the first time, the American Sisters of Charity's black religious garb.

Now Mother Seton moved her religious sisters and the members of her family by stages to Emmitsburg. Her two sons transferred from St. Mary's College in Baltimore to Mount St. Mary's, a Sulpician college in Emmitsburg. Her three daughters, Anna, Catherine, and Rebecca, along with two students from the Paca Street school, as well as her two sisters-in-law, Cecilia Seton, a recent convert to Catholicism, and Harriet Seton, soon to become a Roman Catholic, joined Mother Seton in the new venture. On July 31, the feast of St. Ignatius of Loyola, the American Daughters of Charity, or Sisters of Charity of St. Joseph, as they called themselves, began formal religious life at Emmitsburg. Under the direction of Father DuBourg, the new community established its own religious administration and spiritual program.

Father DuBourg, the sisters' religious director, resigned within the first month, because of a misunderstanding among himself, Mother Seton, and Archbishop Carroll. Father John Baptist David succeeded DuBourg. Within weeks of his appointment, Father David introduced factions, attempted to unseat Mother Seton as superior and supplant her with his own favorite, Sister Rose Landry White, and to change the apostolate of the order from education to hospital work.

A man of tremendous energy and drive, Father David sought to pattern Mother Seton's group directly after the French Sisters of Charity. But Father David met his match in Mother Seton. With fierce determination and skill, she protected her little flock and managed to survive each of Father David's inconsiderate blunders, conducting herself with wisdom, courage, and immense prudence during Father David's two-year mismanagement. She brought her community through its first — and almost last — trial.

But the struggle took its toll. Elizabeth, too, had latent tuberculosis, and now the disease reasserted itself and she felt its pains throughout her body. Harriet Seton, her sister-in-law, died quite unexpectedly at Emmitsburg on December 22, 1809, and within months Cecilia Seton, her other sister-in-law, died. Elizabeth's daughter Anna (Annina), after returning to school in Baltimore, fell in love with a St. Mary's collegian, Charles DuPavillon. DuPavillon jilted the girl, which accelerated her descent into consumption. Anna returned to Emmitsburg, and just before her death on March 12, 1812, took her vows as a member of the Sisters of Charity. Numbed with grief, Elizabeth wrote: "Here I go, like iron or rock, day after day, as he pleases and how he pleases; but to be sure, when my turn comes, I shall be very glad."

A year before Anna's death, Father John Dubois succeeded Father David as the sisters' director. A graduate of the College of Louise-le-Grand, Paris, Dubois had been a classmate of two brutal French revolutionaries, Robespierre and Desmoulins. A man of great energy and ability, Father Dubois fled to America during the French Revolution and began missionary work in Maryland in 1794. As director of the sisters, Dubois rejected union with the French Daughters of Charity and worked to establish the American branch on a firm and independent footing. The priest, who loved to work with his hands, built the "White House," the first school building on the sisters' property. A man of brilliant organization and practical business sense, Father Dubois so constructed the buildings that each room could serve several purposes.

$$*\quad*\quad*\quad*\quad*$$

If Father Dubois provided the practical in Elizabeth's life, another priest, Father Simon Brute, answered her need for the poetic.

As a young man, Simon Gabriel Brute lived through the terror of the French Revolution and graduated as a physician in Paris in 1803. After practicing medicine for a short while, he entered the seminary of St. Sulpice in Paris and became a priest in 1808.

Desiring to serve in the American missions, Brute came to Emmitsburg in 1812 and eventually became Elizabeth's confessor and spiritual director. They communicated in French, which she spoke fluently. Brute, for all his brilliance, never mastered English, probably because that language could never keep up with the rush of his thinking and emotions. A Frenchman to the core, he brought out all Elizabeth's Gallic vitality. Brute, the mystic, lived his life deeply immersed in the presence of the Lord. His spirit of joy and confidence in the heavenly Father's all-powerful care and protection struck a responsive chord in Elizabeth Seton's spirit. He wrote her: "All, all, all, by Providence and in Providence. My

Father Simon Gabriel Brute, Mother Seton's spiritual director, shared with her a vitality, mysticism, and spirit of joy and confidence in the providential presence of God.

Father John Thomas Dubois skillfully guided Mother Seton and her religious community in the early days at Emmitsburg.

Lord! . . . thou didst carry me in thy arms all the days of my life. Oh, let me only trust, abandon myself . . . look at the sky, watch for grace; love and die. Eternity comes next and why not a blessed one through my Jesus? Joy then and again joy."

Father Brute's gentle direction prepared Elizabeth for the final blow that struck in 1816. Her youngest daughter, Rebecca, not yet fourteen, developed a tumor on her hip and died. Elizabeth buried her little Rebecca in the graveyard at Emmitsburg, beside her eldest daughter, Anna. Although the sorrow at parting cut like a sword through her maternal heart, Elizabeth bore the death with great resignation. She wrote to her son William: "It would be too selfish of us to have wished Rebecca's inexpressible sufferings prolonged and her secure bliss deferred for our longer possession...though in her, I have lost the little friend of my heart."

Despite these personal tragedies, Elizabeth pressed on with her lifetime work. Her St. Joseph's Academy at Emmitsburg, serving boarders as well as day pupils from nearby St. Joseph's parish, she saw as a tiny seed which, she hoped, with God's blessing, would someday grow into a mighty tree. Her aim was to encourage religious education for all America's young Catholics.

Dedicated young women crowded the little "White House" to join in the work. These pioneer sisters willingly endured incredible hardships and cold, poverty, uncertainty, and disease. Between 1809 and 1821, nineteen of her sisters and members of her household died — most of tuberculosis. But candidates continued to come. In 1814 in Philadelphia, and in 1817 in New York City, Sister Rose Landry White established the congregation's first orphanages.

*   *   *   *   *

Family troubles plagued Elizabeth down to her grave. Her two sons, William and Richard, resisted all her efforts to establish them in business or professional careers. William finally obtained a commission in the United States Navy, served sixteen years and married into wealth. He lived to an old age, and died a good death, surrounded by his children, among whom was Archbishop Robert Seton. Richard had a way of doing the unexpected. Unsettled and

Chairs like these were used by students in their classrooms in the school at Emmitsburg.

unhappy, he wandered into Emmitsburg as his mother lay dying. He left her on her deathbed just two weeks before she died. In the end he proved he was his Grandfather Bayley's child. Richard died at sea of a fever contracted while nursing a Protestant minister back to health. He was twenty-four years old.

Only one of Elizabeth Seton's children, Catherine Josephine, was with her when she died. Catherine later became a Sister of Mercy and worked in the Tombs prison in New York City for more than fifty years. Until the day she died, Catherine Josephine Seton wore her mother's wedding ring. In her last will she requested that the ring be sent to Emmitsburg to be with her mother's effects.

Elizabeth's health had never been strong since her first apparent bout of tuberculosis in 1804. About 1820 it began to weaken severely. As her final days came, she summed up the story of her life, "I am sick, but not dying; troubled on every side, but not distressed; perplexed, but not despairing; afflicted, but not

With the help of Father Dubois, the sisters built the "White House" on the grounds at Emmitsburg and began conducting America's first parochial school.

forsaken; cast down, but not destroyed; knowing the affliction of this life is but for a moment, for the glory and the life to come will be eternal."

During this last illness Elizabeth again and again manifested her deep love for the eucharist. Once, when a sister offered her medicine to calm her pain, Elizabeth replied: "Never mind the drink. One communion more — then eternity."

As Elizabeth Seton's time ran out, Father Brute noted, "Her tranquility was perfect." The priest asked her: "How are you, Mother?"

"Quiet," she replied — "very quiet."

On January 4, 1821, in the morning's early hours, Elizabeth Seton died. Her last words were the beginning of the prayer of Pius VII. "May the most just, the most high, and most amiable will of God be in all things fulfilled, praised and exalted forever."

Father Brute wrote to Antonio Filicchi of the woman they both loved. "Near home we deposited her precious remains on the day following her death. In this little woods she reposes with about fifteen sisters and novices who had come to join her. She leaves more than fifty sisters who survive her to follow in her footsteps — forty of them at St. Joseph's, the others at the Mountain [Mount St. Mary's College], in Philadelphia and New York. She lived only for her sisters and for the performance of her holy duties.... Her heart was compassionate, religious, lavish of every good in her possession, disinterested in regard to all other things. O Mother, excellent Mother, I trust you are now in the enjoyment of bliss."

Six congregations of North American Sisters of Charity trace their origins back to Mother Elizabeth Seton, shown here in the order's original habit.

In 1907 James Cardinal Gibbons of Baltimore commissioned an examination of Elizabeth Seton's life, works, and writings, and in 1939 her cause was formally introduced in Rome. On March 17, 1963, Pope John XXIII beatified Mother Seton.

Five months later a significant cure took place. Carl Kalin, sixty-one years old, the Protestant husband of a Catholic wife, was brought into St. Joseph's Hospital in Yonkers, New York, at 6:00 p.m., suffering from meningoencephalitis, complicated by red measles — a fatal combination. By 9:00 he was suffering convulsions, was in a coma, and had turned black. The nun in charge of the case, a Sister of Charity, called the Motherhouse at Mount St. Vincent, New York, where a novena was started while a relic of Blessed Elizabeth Seton was applied to the patient. On the third day extraordinary things began to happen that the doctor in charge described as "the point where theology takes over." Kalin's temperature dropped, convulsions ceased, and he came out of the coma and cheerily greeted his wife.

In 1973, Mr. Kalin underwent a complete medical checkup, and it was found that he had no residual effects from his extraordinary illness. He was later received into the Catholic church and was present at Mother Seton's canonization by Paul VI on September 14, 1975. Her feast is observed on January 4. She is the United States' first native-born saint.

Jeanne Jugan

"Ah, Mademoiselle, I do not understand!"

"But, Monsieur Leroy, there is little to understand."

"You, Mademoiselle Jugan, wish to leave my employ. You are an excellent servant. Do you wish more money? Do you wish shorter hours? You have been a joy to my family. France is plagued with monstrous unemployment, and now you tell me you do not wish to work any more."

"I did not say I do not wish to work any more, Monsieur," the forty-seven-year-old woman responded. "I told you, I wish to serve the poor in our town."

"But what can you who are so poor yourself do for the poor of Saint-Servan?"

The interrogator's voice and face betrayed his exasperation. His normally ruddy complexion ripened into deep purple; his pale-blue eyes flashed; his golden-white mustachios bristled. Monsieur Leroy looked like a sleek old tomcat about to pounce.

"I am not sure what I can do for the poor," the woman answered calmly.

"And where," Leroy pressed on sarcastically, "are you going to find means to feed Saint-Servan's hoard of starvelings?"

The maidservant gazed at him a moment and replied, "From people like you, Monsieur Leroy."

The old man bowed his head. The woman had gained the advantage.

"I intend to collect from door to door and offer shelter to whomever I can, particularly the aged poor. You are a kind man, Monsieur. I know you will help me."

"You are a good woman, Jeanne." For the first time he used her Christian name. He reached into his pocket and pulled out a wad of franc notes. "Take these, and God bless you." He pressed three hundred francs into her hand. It was a substantial sum for the times and in Brittany could purchase a large amount of food.

Leroy's temper had cooled; his face broke into a contagious grin. "Mademoiselle," he said, "God has given you the grace of asking." The old man threw back his head as a rich, melodious laugh rolled up from deep inside him and filled the morning with joy.

*   *   *   *   *

Jeanne Jugan was born October 25, 1792, at Petites-Croix, Cancale, a picturesque fishing village perched atop the great cliffs overlooking the Bay of Mont Saint-Michel in Brittany, France. She was the sixth of the eight children of Joseph Jugan (originally spelled Joucan) and Marie Horel.

For the Jugans, as for all Bretons, life was hard, as hard as the massive stone bluffs that rose from the bay and stood like the folded fists of giant Druid gods in its cold green waters. Suffering, death, poverty, and illness were never

Jeanne was born and raised in this humble one-room cottage in Brittany.

strangers in the land. Brittany's men earned their livelihood from the soil and the sea. While the ocean gave life, it also claimed life mercilessly and regularly.

One of its victims was Jeanne's father, lost at sea when she was three and a half years old. Her mother, with steadfast purpose and total dedication, struggled through years of war, famine, and plague to keep her family together in the warmth and cheerfulness of their one-room, earthen-floored cottage.

* * * * *

France, unable to exorcise its inner demons, writhed in torment at the end of the eighteenth and beginning of the nineteenth centuries.

The Revolution of 1789 affected the very character of the French soul and set in motion forces destructive to the nation's oldest institutions — the monarchy, the nobility, the peasantry, and the church. The Bretons, devout Catholics, watched in horror as officials and supporters of the atheistic and anticlerical regime hounded, harassed, and murdered priests and religious, and displaced priests loyal to Rome with others who subscribed to the Civil Constitution of the Clergy of 1790. On the local level, Bretons witnessed the conversion of their parish church into a hospital and a military storehouse.

As the eighteenth century ended, peasants and Royalists alike, recoiling from the first shock of the Revolution, took up arms against its leaders. Civil war flared throughout the land. Fierce fighting broke out in Brittany and in its deadly train came famine, disease, and disorder. Military deserters and beggars ran like packs of starved rats through the countryside, pillaging, murdering, and raping. Armed forces of both sides plundered farms and villages, torturing and executing the hapless population.

From Cancale's harbor, Jeanne's father sailed off to sea for the last time.

Death's specter lurked everywhere as the bloody waves of revolution and counter-revolution convulsed the land.

The people of Brittany stuck together and supported each other in the face of calamity. Women who had lived with the tradition of sudden death as the sea claimed husbands, sons, and brothers over the centuries responded with customary strength to the challenges of disaster overtaking their beautiful peninsula. They fed and clothed each other, shared their bread, nurtured their infants, nursed their sick, and buried their dead. These confident, sturdy women had little time for self-pity or tears.

Breton peasants, especially the women, firmly believed in a God who would eventually set things right, and the impact of civil war failed to shake their strong faith. No anticlerical government could thwart their firm determination to express their faith publicly. Despite laws forbidding public devotions, the

women of Cancale, for instance, fasting and in silence, walked each dawn to the tiny, tumbledown chapel of "Our Lady of the Orchard." There, before a plaster statue of the Virgin, they recited the rosary, praying for their husbands, sons, and brothers. Jeanne and her mother took part in the morning devotions.

The courage, resourcefulness, and fidelity of the women of Brittany and other parts of France in the face of persecutions and death profoundly affected the young Jeanne Jugan. Among the bravest of them ranked a band of women called the "Trotting Sisters." Their official title was the Third Order of the Heart of the Admirable Mother.

The revolutionary government, which had banned religious orders,

Jeanne and her mother prayed daily at this tiny chapel dedicated to Our Lady of the Orchard, standing sentinel on Cancale's wind-swept shore.

had hundreds of priests, nuns, and brothers executed and drove thousands more into exile. Some French priests and religious went underground, concealing their identity, wearing secular clothing, living as lay people in small homes, apartments, or cottages, meeting together only in greater secrecy, and carrying on clandestine forms of ministry.

The "Trotting Sisters," so called because they had no established convents and were constantly on the move in their ministry, were despised by the government and had a price on their heads. Despite prohibitions of the regime, they continued their work of teaching catechism to French children. From them, as well as from her mother, Jeanne learned the rudiments and love of Catholic faith and practice.

*   *   *   *   *

When Jeanne was about sixteen years of age, she hired herself out as a kitchen maid on an estate in the nearby Breton village of St. Coulomb. Her employer, the Viscountess de la Choue, possessed a generous heart and ordered the young maid to be kind to the numerous beggars who visited her well-stocked kitchen. She appointed Jeanne to accompany her on their customary visits to the sick and poor on and around her estate. Jeanne never forgot the noblewoman's delicate sensitivity. "Treat the poor only as you yourself would wish to be treated," she counseled. "The food we bring must be offered with the deepest respect and love." Besides providing Jeanne with an example of truly Christian charity, the Viscountess cultivated in the young lady a certain refinement of manners, not ordinarily found among those of the peasant class.

Inevitably a young Breton sailor fell head over heels in love with Jeanne and, without any encouragement from her, proposed marriage. She declined the offer twice in as many years. She told him: "I cannot marry you. I am not sure yet what God wants me to do with my life, but I cannot become your wife."

Jeanne apparently joined the "Trotting Sisters" when she was about twenty-five years of age. To support herself, she took a job at the Hospital du Rosais in Saint-Servan.

Saint-Servan, a seaport near Cancale, had a population of about ten thousand people, four thousand of whom city authorities registered as beggars. Prior to Jeanne's arrival, military disaster along with political unrest and famine had

Merchants and sea captains built magnificent mansions in the area. Jeanne, in her early teens, served as a maid in this stately home.

combined to visit large-scale misery on the town. The hospital represented the feeble attempt of city officials to cope with the needs of the port's immense crowd of sick and starving people. The hospital bakery provided scores of loaves of cheap bread made from potato flour for distribution to the needy. Jeanne worked in the hospital dispensary and did bedside nursing.

Jeanne expended all her physical and mental resources on the overwhelming work at the hospital. At the end of six years, exhausted in mind and spirit, she skidded toward a complete breakdown. She had to leave her job.

Mademoiselle Lecoq, a gentle woman of comfortable means who lived opposite the Church of Sainte-Croix in Saint-Servan, asked Jeanne to enter her employ. So fatigued was Jeanne that she could hardly fulfill her duties; so generous was Mademoiselle Lecoq that she cheerfully cared for Jeanne. In a reversal of roles the lady, who may have been a "Trotting Sister," spent more time waiting on the maid than the maid on the lady. She insisted that Jeanne receive proper food and medicine. Each day the two women spent hours in silent prayer and attended Mass. They also conducted catechetical instruction for children in the town.

Brittany's potato crop failed in 1826, followed by failure of the cereal crop three years later. France and England were both plunged into financial depression. Laborers and factory workers joined starving and dispossessed farmers roaming the countryside. Desperate predators in search of food once again ravaged Brittany with riots, arson, murder, and rape. Mademoiselle Lecoq and Jeanne labored ceaselessly to care for the poor and other unfortunate people. The sixty-three-year-old Mademoiselle Lecoq broke under the strain and died. Jeanne lost her dearest friend.

Alone once more, Jeanne Jugan begged God to show her her life's work. Time was running out. She was forty-three years of age and still unsure of what God wanted of her.

This rare photograph shows the streets of Saint-Servan at the time Jeanne Jugan encountered the sufferings of the town's poor and elderly.

Jeanne, at the age of forty-seven, began her life's work in this second floor apartment in Saint-Servan, which she shared with two other women.

In 1837, Jeanne, with seventy-two-year-old Francoise Aubert, rented the second story and two-room attic of a humble cottage near the Church of Sainte-Croix. Francoise, retired, still earned a few pennies by spinning. Jeanne continued to hire out. The two women formed a community of prayer, catechized children, and assisted the poor. They were joined before long by Virginie Tredaniel, a seventeen-year-old orphan dressmaker. The three earned enough to feed, clothe, and shelter themselves. Whatever they had left over they gave to the poor.

The dark spirits of hunger, famine, disease, and epidemic refused to depart from Saint-Servan. The face of the poor was everywhere. No one could escape it and no one could make it disappear.

What was true of Saint-Servan was true of all Europe and the industrial areas of America. "It is a disgrace to our civilization," Prince Louis-Napoleon Bonaparte wrote, "when you think that in the nineteenth century one-tenth of the population is in rags and dying of hunger." The prince blamed the situation on the Industrial Revolution. "Industry is a machine functioning without a regulator," he complained. "Indifferently it grinds up men and material in its wheels, depopulating the countryside, crowding people into airless slums, weakening the spirit and body alike and ultimately, when having no further use for them, throwing on to the street those who have sacrificed their strength, their youth, their very existence to create industrial wealth."

*   *   *   *   *

Just as a great symphony begins with a single note, a great work of art with one stroke of the brush, and a great literary masterpiece with one word, so Jeanne at the age of forty-seven began her life's work with one decision. She determined to devote all her energy and time to serving the poor. It was this decision that prompted her famous conversation with Monsieur Leroy. With the approval of Francoise and Virginie, she turned her attention to the most pitiful of the poor — the aged, abandoned ladies she met every day in the town square, huddling against cold walls, seeking shelter from wintry blasts, and begging food and wine from women shopping in the market. Near the end of 1839, a cruel year, she invited Anne Chauvin, a blind widow, to share their apartment. "I will bring Anne home," Jeanne told her companions; and, remembering what she

Jeanne and Virginie Tredaniel gave their own beds to their first two elderly guests.

"Little Sisters, take good care of the aged, for in them you are caring for Jesus himself." This painting by James Collison (1825–1881) shows the loving service Jeanne taught her Little Sisters of the Poor.

had learned of hospitality from the Viscountess de la Choue, she added, "as I would bring my own mother." Jeanne gave her bed to Anne and moved from the second-floor apartment to the attic. She was joined there a few days later by Virginie, who gave up her bed to Isabelle Coeuru, the household's second elderly guest.

Virginie, who continued her outside employment, assisted Jeanne in performing the multiple tasks — cleaning, washing, cooking, serving — involved in caring for the two elderly women. Francoise did her bit with good cheer and earned a little money with her knitting and spinning.

Within a short time two young women, Marie Jamet and Madeleine Bourges, began visiting the little hospice and volunteering their services. Jeanne devised a simple regimen for them, Virginie, and herself, based on the rule of life of the "Trotting Sisters." Francoise, in her middle seventies, felt that the requirements of the rule were beyond her. She was content to pray, spin, and smile.

The twenty-eight-year-old curate of Saint-Servan, Father Auguste Le Pailleur, served as spiritual director and confessor for the nascent community.

*   *   *   *   *

Jeanne and her companions needed more room for themselves and their guests by the summer of 1841. For one hundred francs a year they rented an abandoned bar close to Saint-Servan's harbor, which featured a room large enough to accommodate a dozen beds and two smaller rooms for the staff and storage. A neighbor offered the use of a room for a chapel. Seventy-five-year-old Francoise became chief housekeeper. Jeanne continued her collecting tours. Madeleine, Virginie, and Marie used the wages they earned to support the household.

A young lady who visited the new place of residence wrote:

> There was a big downstairs room where seats were few but the beds, in contrast, were very close together. I made myself small on a stool between two cots, the blankets of which were made up of countless numbers of scraps. I saw Jeanne Jugan; she was getting ready to go out collecting; she was putting on her cloak and adjusting her hood. Over her arm she put her basket, already such a well-known sight in all the town.

The old women called her Sister Jeanne. "Sister Jeanne," they would say, "do our job properly for us, collect for us; don't forget our errands, our tobacco and our pennies."

Jeanne would lean over them, listening to a few more whispered instructions. She smiled at them. I am fairly sure she kissed one or two of the old women — the blind ones perhaps. She left them promptly for she did things quickly yet never gave the impression of hurrying or being hurried. I was impressed by the cleanliness reigning in this large, rather dark room, and also by the way the poor furniture was arranged.

When we left, my sister said to me, "Did you notice how well those old women are being looked after and how happy they look?"

Three months after opening these quarters, which people called "The Big Downstairs," Jeanne needed even larger accommodations. She got them with acquisition of the former convent of the Daughters of the Cross which had been confiscated by the government following the suppression of religious orders. Assisting her were Mademoiselle Doynel, a tradeswoman, and Father Le Pailleur,

Jeanne purchased an abandoned convent in Saint-Servan and called it the Home of the Cross. The Sisters still use the building today for care of the elderly.

along with many others whose contributions eventually covered the purchase price of twenty thousand francs.

The new Home of the Cross was Jeanne's first outpost, her first major advance in her personal war on poverty. The building was in good condition but needed some adaptions for its new purpose. Jeanne, her ladies, and generous-hearted Bretons, rich and poor, threw their energies into the renovations. One of her first workers was Monsieur Brisart, a policeman who moonlighted as a carpenter. He converted old church pews into bunks for the residents. Doctor Blaichier, an old friend from the Hospital du Rosais, volunteered medical services. Forty-four "good women," as Jeanne described her elderly guests, resided at the home in dignity and cheer. During the winter of 1842–43, Jeanne welcomed the first male guest to the residence in the person of seventy-five-year-old Rodolphe Laisne, a blind, half-dead, and abandoned sailor. Under her care and that of her companions, he lived at the home into his eighties.

Not everyone in Saint-Servan applauded Jeanne's work. Civil welfare authorities, chagrined by her purchase of the imposing Home of the Cross, accused her of megalomania and cut off gifts of clothing they had previously supplied for its residents. Others, judging that the peasant woman had overstepped her bounds with her grandiose project, refused to contribute to its support.

Despite these reverses, Jeanne continued her begging. A proud woman in whom haughty Breton blood flowed, she bridled inwardly at asking anything of anybody. But she had identified herself

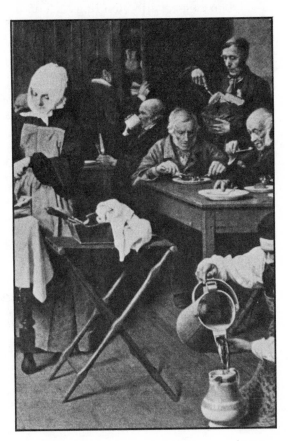

Jeanne established a special accomodation for men in Saint-Servan. Breton sailors were among Jeanne's most generous benefactors and she delighted in caring for the elderly mariners.

with her old folks. They were her mothers and fathers, and she would struggle despite personal cost to provide for them the warmth, hospitality, and love that mothers and fathers justly deserved. Her whole spirit of generosity and dedication proved so moving that the rich and poor of Saint-Servan joined their efforts to hers. Even wealthy women found themselves begging assistance from whomever they could to raise funds for Jeanne's work. The bishop visited the Home of the Cross and gave his public blessing to Jeanne and her apostolate, thereby squelching opposition in some Catholic quarters. Saint-Servan's shipyard workers, poor but gracious, gave Jeanne a penny or two each pay day.

In September, 1844, a visitor to the Home of the Cross wrote: "I visited a room where the women assemble to unpick old rope to make oakum for caulking the ships. The room is large and square in shape, with chairs along all the four walls. Complete silence reigns and a sweet serenity plays on every face. It has taken great effort to bring each of these poor creatures, whom society had rejected and whose conduct was frequently bad, to this regular, hard-working way of life. One's admiration is redoubled when one reflects that this good order had been brought about by the agency of five or six young women. . . . The finger of God is in it."

The bad conduct to which the writer referred was drinking, to which elderly Bretons were prone. Older people, thrown out in the cold and damp streets, found their only relief in alcohol. Jeanne never made an issue of their wine drinking but simply offered them clean, warm surroundings, and more importantly, love and respect. In short order, they got their drinking under control.

A document describing Jeanne's work and signed by the leading citizens of Saint-Servan was submitted to the prestigious French Academy in 1845. The purpose of the presentation was to seek the Montyon Prize awarded by the Academy "to reward a poor French man or women for outstandingly meritorious activity." Jeanne received the prize late in the year and immediately applied its award — the equivalent of seven hundred dollars — to the support of her apostolate.

Even the bitterly anti-Catholic Freemasons honored Jeanne — with a gold medal that she had melted down and reshaped into the cup of a chalice for use at Mass.

*   *   *   *   *

In 1842 and again in 1843, Jeanne and her companions met with Father Le Pailleur to further define their religious association. The women took vows of poverty, chastity, and obedience and added a fourth, hospitality. Jeanne was elected superior in both years.

On December 23, 1843, two weeks after a second organizational meeting and second election of Jeanne as superior, Father Le Pailleur summoned the four nuns, nullified the election on his own authority, and appointed Marie Jamet Superior General in place of Jeanne.

Jeanne accepted this development without complaint. In later years, though, she remarked to Father Le Pailleur: "You have stolen my work from me, but I willingly relinquish it to you!"

In the following year the four women chose a new name for their community, Little Sisters of the Poor, and adopted religious names for themselves.

Jeanne's name was Sister Mary of the Cross, but people continued to call her Jeanne Jugan and referred to her companions as "Little Jeanne Jugans."

Jeanne lost no opportunity to recruit candidates for the community, but vocations came slowly at first. Most young Breton women recoiled from the ceaseless work and poor lives of the "Little Jeanne Jugans."

In January, 1846, Jeanne established a second home in Rennes, a large city close to Saint-Servan. Reporting on the event, the local journal said:

> She is the image of charity on earth. She told us about the great stroke of luck that she had. A little while ago she had taken three new

In January, 1846, Jeanne traveled to the neighboring city of Rennes to collect for the home at Saint-Servan. In February, she opened this home in Rennes itself.

invalids into her house. One of them had only a filthy hole to live in!
The others had not slept in a bed for twenty years! Jeanne and two
of her assistants had to turn out to make room for the newcomers.

"Jeanne, but where did you and your companions sleep?" we
asked.

"On the floor," she responded. "But wasn't it hard?" we queried. "We never noticed. . . ." she replied.

Rennes, like the rest of France, was in the grip of financial depression
when the Little Sisters arrived. A year later, severe rioting broke out in the city.
Citizens pillaged grain ships in the harbor, broke into bakeries, and attacked the
police. Despite the disorders, Jeanne's work flourished. In her inimitable way,
she involved many leading citizens in her work. One volunteer, the manager of
the government's optic telegraph, Monsieur Varangot, applied his considerable
carpentry skills to improve the home at Rennes.

The Little Sisters continued to enjoy God's favors in their new home. One
time as they were about to boil water for a huge pile of laundry, they found their
supply of firewood exhausted. "We had no wood," a nun remembered, "so we
did the only thing we could; we prayed. Soon a cart full of wood came along.
The driver told us that his master had come into his yard a short while before
and said, 'Make up a cart load of wood for the Little Sisters.' And, as the driver
was getting ready to load the wood, his master came back and said: 'The Sisters
are so poor that they won't be able to pay anyone to chop it up for them. Take
it already chopped.'"

On another occasion after the sisters had fed all their residents and gathered
for their own meal, there was nothing left for them to eat. Jeanne told the sister
refectorian to ring the bell signalling dinner time anyway. "At least that way,"
she said, "we will observe the Rule."

"We went into the dining room," a Little Sister recalled. "After we said
our grace, we began our usual reading. Someone rang the front doorbell. A nun
promptly answered the door and returned to the dining room, trembling. A rich
person's servant had arrived, loaded down, bringing a complete supper for all
the sisters. Nothing was missing."

*   *   *   *   *

The report of Jeanne's activity presented to the French Academy described her familiar figure as she passed through the towns of Brittany:

> She is forever on the go, whatever the weather, with a basket over her arm, and this she always brings home full . . . .
>
> In pleading their cause [of the poor] she is truly eloquent. She has often been known to burst into tears when explaining their needs. And so it is hard to refuse her, and she has nearly always succeeded in melting even the hardest of hearts . . . .
>
> She has truly thrown in her lot with the poor; she dresses like them in what she is given; she lives on leftovers as they do, always making a point to keep the best bits for those who are sick or more infirm; and the persons assisting her copy her example.

    *   *   *   *   *

Father Le Pailleur and the sisters further refined the Rule of Life in May, 1846. This latest version reflected the influence of the Hospital Brothers of St. John of God, whose Father Felix Massot greatly admired Jeanne and guided her in developing a spirituality for her sisters.

Father Le Pailleur inserted in the new text his right to rule: "The Father General will enjoy all the same rights as are enjoyed by the Mother Superior General, and furthermore the latter will submit to and obey him in all things." Mother Superior General and Father Superior General were both equal, but Father Superior General was more equal.

Jeanne established her third home in the nearby city of Dinan in an abandoned prison built into the city wall.

In that same year Jeanne opened a third foundation in the city of Dinan at the site of a former prison built into the city wall. An English visitor, thought to be Charles Dickens, subsequently wrote about her:

> To reach the floor where they were living, you had to negotiate an awkward spiral stair, the ceiling of the room was low, the walls were bare and rough, the windows narrow and grilled, so that you might have imagined you were in a cavern or prison; but this dismal look was to some extent enlivened by the firelight and the happy appearance of the people inside. . . . Jeanne received us kindly. She was simply but cleanly dressed in a black dress and white cap and kerchief; this is the dress adopted by the community. She looks about fifty years old, is of medium height with a sunburnt complexion. She looks worn out though her expression is serene and full of kindness; there is not the slightest trace of pretentiousness or conceit detectable in it.

So successful was Jeanne in soliciting alms that a French newspaper observed: "Visiting charitable people, she merely says, 'I am Jeanne Jugan.' The name alone is enough to open all purses."

Another writer noted: "There is something so calm, so holy about this woman that, seeing her, I felt as though I were in the presence of a higher being, and her words went so much to my heart that my eyes — I know not why — filled with tears."

When Jeanne met with a refusal, she accepted it graciously, thanked the person, and, without further ado, left. She also had the knack of knowing just when to press her case.

Once she was begging on a wharf when longshoremen unloading a large shipment of gold ingots dropped one worth about ten thousand francs into the water. The ship owner who had purchased the ingots saw the accident and exploded. Jeanne knew him and tried to calm him. "I'll pray, Monsieur," she promised, "that you find your ingot." The merchant turned the palms of his hands heavenward and continued his verbal explosion. Jeanne left to continue her begging.

The longshoremen later retrieved the ingot from the bottom of the bay. When Jeanne returned to the pier, she met the merchant clutching his precious bar in both hands.

"I told you, Monsieur, that God would help you recover your money!" she said, and laughed quietly.

The owner handed her the ingot, saying: "Take it Jeanne. This is for your old folks!"

*   *   *   *   *

By the summer of 1851, more than one hundred sisters were in the congregation and ten houses had been established for the aged poor. Five more houses were founded and two hundred more sisters were in the institute by the end of the year, when the total number of residents under care was approximately fifteen hundred. Formal episcopal approval of the institute was granted by Bishop Brossais Saint-Marc of Rennes in May, 1852. Papal approbation was given by Pius IX twenty-six months later, when the community had five hundred sisters engaged in the care of the aged poor in thirty-six houses.

During her last years, Jeanne worked in the convent sewing room, where young postulants and novices listened to her loving and cheerful words of wisdom, unaware that she had founded their order.

Father Le Pailleur, in full control of the Little Sisters as their Father Superior General, made an incredible decision in 1852. He summoned the indefatigable Jeanne to the motherhouse at Rennes and told her she was no longer to collect alms for the Little Sisters. "You are not to maintain any contact with benefactors," he decreed. "And," he added, "you are to remain in a hidden life behind the walls of the motherhouse." He appointed her to supervise the manual work of the postulants.

Jeanne obeyed without complaint. She died twenty-seven years later. Her visible mission on earth, the founding of the Little Sisters of the Poor, was finished. It had consumed but twelve years of her life.

Father Superior General rewrote the history of the Little Sisters of the Poor. He described himself as their founder and Jeanne only as an auxiliary. He gradually revised the official history until her name was eradicated. So successful was the effort that postulants and novices with whom Jeanne lived, worked, and prayed at the motherhouse had no idea she was the foundress of the institute they had joined.

Father Le Pailleur served the sisters well for many years, but in time his imagination ran away with him. He began to believe that he had actually originated their institute and apostolate. In his view, he was the founder and chief executive of the immense effort. He convinced himself that he had met the first poor women and had engineered the great miracle of charity. Ultimately, his fantasy world became his real world, about which Cardinal Garrone commented:

> We . . . see the extraordinary state of affairs where the found-
> ress universally recognized as such and brought into the public
> eye as the recipient of a . . . national award [the Montyon Prize],
> and so famous even abroad that foreigners come specially to see
> her, is simultaneously pushed into the background within her own
> community, one humble servant among many others, condemned
> to obscure tasks and only called back to light when a foundation
> is on the verge of collapse, which by her reputation and personal
> gifts she instantly and miraculously restores to health.

As the order continued to grow, the novitiate at Rennes proved to be too small. A new motherhouse and novitiate were acquired in 1856 at Saint-Perm, north of Rennes. The sisters called their new home "St. Joseph's Tower." A

large estate, the property eventually
accommodated six hundred novices
and postulants. Father Le Pailleur sent
Jeanne there in 1856. He exploited the
occasion by directing fresh insults at
her. He ended her supervision of the
manual work of postulants and left her
without any assignment to specific
duties.

Expansion of the institute beyond
the borders of France had begun by this
time, to England and Belgium, and subsequently resulted in the establishment
of houses also in Spain, Ireland, the
United States, North Africa, Italy, and
other places. The chief architect of this
expansion was Father Ernest Lelievre,
scion of a family of industrialists in
northern France, a doctor of law and
theology. He became acquainted with
the work of the Little Sisters through
the St. Vincent de Paul Society and
subsequently devoted his considerable
energy, intellect, influence, and financial resources into establishing homes
of the Little Sisters in various places to
which he traveled.

Father Lelievre held Jeanne in
high regard and liked to keep her informed of his journeys. She, although
ordinarily reticent to speak about herself or her problems, seemed to be

In 1856 the order acquired a new
motherhouse and novitiate at Saint-
Perm, which they called St. Joseph's Tower.

very much at ease with him. She told him about her concern over her heart shortly after Father Le Pailleur had ordered her to stay in the motherhouse.

"I've got something the matter with my heart," she said. "I can't last long. I am ready to go."

"Don't you worry, Sister," he replied; "you aren't going to die yet. I shouldn't be alarmed."

As it turned out, Jeanne's heart kept beating for twenty-five more years.

By 1870, seventy-eight-year-old Jeanne had quarters in the infirmary of the motherhouse, close to the choir loft of the chapel. Despite the pain of an ulcerated leg, she often walked slowly and with difficulty from her room to the loft where she prayed for hours before the Blessed Sacrament.

She maintained absolute discretion about the wrong that had been done to her. She never complained. She made no effort to correct Father Le Pailleur's history of the Little Sisters. She kept in lively spirits and was always ready to smile, laugh, and break into song. The young nuns loved her.

The novices and postulants found her a never-failing source of encouragement. When they brought their troubles to her, she would often say, "Go, take a walk. Fresh air will blow the troubles out of your mind." She worried about their health. "Your health is not your own," she counseled. "It is a gift from God himself, to help you serve his poor."

One Little Sister remembered: "When I was a brand new postulant, Sister Mary of the Cross used to call me 'her little acolyte.' She was thoroughly concerned about everything. One morning when it was time for examination

of conscience, I was coming back from pulling up cabbage stalks. Sister Mary of the Cross saw that I was dripping with sweat; she sent me off to change so that I wouldn't catch cold."

"Go and find Jesus," she advised the young nuns, "when your patience and strength give out and you feel alone and helpless. He is waiting for you in the chapel. Say to him, 'Jesus, you know exactly what is going on. You are all I have, and you know

Taken in 1870 or 1871, this is the only known photograph of Jeanne Jugan, Sister Mary of the Cross.

all. Come to my help.' And then go and don't worry about how you are going to manage. That you have told God about it is enough. He has a good memory."

She shared her meditations with the novices. "Think, little ones," she said one time, "how dearly all three members of the Holy Family loved one another! How happy they looked! How kindly, how gently they spoke to one another! In our little family, we must do the same. . . . The Blessed Virgin was poor, too. She did as the poor do. She never wasted her time, for the poor cannot afford to sit idle; and in this we should imitate the Holy Family."

"Little ones," she also used to say, "you must always be cheerful! Our little old people do not like long faces."

Because of her bad leg, she used a gnarled walking stick. From time to time the young nuns would see her walking alone in the woods and waving the stick as though she were conducting an invisible orchestra. She would sing aloud, cheerfully and joyfully.

*   *   *   *   *

Jeanne was eighty-six years old in 1878. She was just above medium height, very thin, and half-blind. Her carriage remained erect. Her eyelids were half-closed due to nerve deterioration, but her eyes continued to reflect cheer and joy.

In March, 1879, when Pope Leo XIII approved the constitutions of the institute for a seven-year trial period, the community numbered 2,400 Little Sisters.

As spring blended into summer, Jeanne grew weaker and weaker. Toward the end of August, she took to her bed. She lost consciousness and was given the Sacrament of the Sick. When awake, she prayed: "Oh Mary, you know you are my Mother. Do not forsake me! . . . You know I love you and how I long to see you!" These were her last words.

People remembered that even in death the face of Jeanne Jugan was full of calmness and peace, reflecting the presence of God.

Jeanne was buried in the order's graveyard at the motherhouse. Nothing at her gravesite indicated her crucial role in the history of the Little Sisters. Father Le Pailleur engraved on her tombstone the notice that Sister Mary of the Cross was the third woman to enter the Little Sisters of the Poor.

As the years went on, Father Le Pailleur grew more bizarre in his conduct. He insisted on displays of adulation from the Little Sisters. Wielding absolute authority, he governed every phase of the institute's activities. He judged the suitability of candidates, the courses of studies, the location of new foundations. Authorities in Rome gradually became aware of the strange occurrences in Brittany and instituted an investigation. In 1890, eleven years after Jeanne's death and when Father Le Pailleur was seventy-eight years old, church officials removed him from office and brought him to Rome where he ended his days in a convent.

Marie Jamet, the Mother Superior General and most pitiful victim of Father Le Pailleur's megalomania, told bystanders at her deathbed: "I am not the first Little Sister, nor the foundress of the work. Jeanne Jugan was the first one and the foundress of the Little Sisters of the Poor." Jeanne was beatified on October 3, 1982, and her feast is observed on August 30.

In March, 1936, Little Sisters removed Jeanne's remains from the convent graveyard to a crypt beneath the chapel.

Elizabeth of the Trinity

From the sacristy doorway, the priest conducting the parish mission for women at St. Hilaire, France, that early winter of 1882 surveyed the congregation. Mothers and their little ones were in the church for the blessing of children. The priest, who always enjoyed this tender ceremony, spotted Marie Catez and her nineteen-month-old daughter, Elizabeth, side by side in the front pew. Earlier in the afternoon while Elizabeth napped, her mother had loaned her favorite doll, Jeanette, to the priest for use in the blessing ceremony.

"I will so disguise Jeanette," the priest assured Marie, "that your Elizabeth will never recognize her. I will place the doll in a crib in the sanctuary, dress it like the Baby Jesus, and surround it with candles and flowers." Although Marie did not share the priest's certainty that he could so easily deceive her daughter, she handed over Jeanette.

The priest glanced at Elizabeth as he entered the sanctuary to begin the ceremony. "Such a sweet child," he thought.

The "sweet child," sitting placidly beside her mother, moved her sparkling

123

black eyes slowly across the sanctuary. The statues of the angels and saints, the crucifix, the flickering candles entranced her. As the priest entered the sanctuary, her gaze fastened on the crib. Suddenly, her placid face darkened, her eyes narrowed. She tugged at her mother's coat and pointed to the crib. "That's my Jeanette!" she cried out in a loud voice. Marie put a finger to her lips. "Shh," she said.

Elizabeth emitted a wail that filled the sanctuary vault and drowned out the priest's prayers. "That's my Jeanette!" she bellowed.

"How," wondered the priest, "can such a tiny body generate such volume?"

"You took my Jeanette, bad priest!" the child shouted. "Bad priest, bad priest!" she howled.

The priest, interrupting his prayers, turned toward Marie and shrugged. She seized the twisting, shouting child in her arms and rushed out the church door.

Although the rapidity with which Elizabeth penetrated her doll's disguise surprised Marie, her firstborn's temper tantrums did not. She had endured their fury before. Within months of this incident, she wrote to her husband, Captain Joseph Catez, who was away on military

Elizabeth Catez, with her doll Jeannette, amazed everyone with her energetic and tempestuous personality.

Marie Catez, a determined woman, needed all the strength she could muster to raise her precocious and stubborn daughter.

Captain Joseph Catez, a much decorated cavalry officer, deeply loved his family. He died of a heart attack when Elizabeth was seven years old.

maneuvers: "Elizabeth is a real devil; she is crawling and needs a pair of pants every day."

Despite her rages, Elizabeth brought deep joy to her father, a Knight of the French Legion of Honor, and her mother.

Joseph Francis Catez, a raw, twenty-one-year-old French farmer, enlisted in the French Army in 1853. He soldiered in Algeria and Italy for about ten years and later, during the Franco-Prussian War of 1870, spent seven months as a prisoner. After the cessation of hostilities, he earned the rank of lieutenant in the cavalry. Several years later, he met Marie Rolland, daughter of Cavalry Commandant Raymond Rolland. They were married September 3, 1879.

Elizabeth was born July 18, 1880, at Camp D'Avor. Healthy, energetic, and self-willed, the baby soon proved as formidable as a cavalry charge. Marie,

Elizabeth was born July 18, 1880, in this house at the military post in D'Avor. Her mother (center) holds the baby; her father, holding a riding crop, stands to the right.

bearing warriors' blood in her own veins, proved equal to Elizabeth's tantrums. Precocious and loquacious, the child often demonstrated ill temper at table. Such displays earned exile to her room. Locked there, the tiny beauty kicked the door and hurled around the room whatever articles she could seize. Such behavior merited further discipline. Marie most effectively punished her tiny wildcat by refusing her a good-night kiss.

Two and a half years after Elizabeth's birth, when the Catezes were stationed at the Dijon military base, their second child, Marguerite, was born. Gentle, calm, and placid, she offered Marie some relief. "Elizabeth often went into rages," Marguerite recalled in later years. "They were quite terrible. Her eyes would flash furiously." But the younger sister also remembered Elizabeth as cheerful and generous. Her mother remembered: "She delighted in talking, she was a chatterbox." Playmates recalled her as "warm, friendly, cheerful."

Withal, the family was happy. A letter from Marie to her husband, away on military maneuvers, affords a glimpse into the love the parents had for each other. "Dear Joseph, do not forget my advice; take care of yourself; do not drink too much beer or smoke too many cigars; take care of your health and think of us."

Marie's concern came from her awareness that Joseph had developed heart trouble. Two years after retiring from the army, he suffered a fatal heart attack at age fifty-five. Marie then faced the challenge of bringing up two daughters, seven-year-old Elizabeth and five-year-old Marguerite, without the father they all loved so deeply.

Marie moved to a modest house outside the Dijon military base and reorganized her family life. An army pension enabled her and the two girls to live decently. She arranged for Elizabeth to begin piano and French lessons. Although so tiny she could hardly reach the pedals, Elizabeth attacked the piano

Gentle mild-mannered Marguerite, born two and a half years after Elizabeth, gave her mother a welcome respite. In later years she recalled her sister's cheerful and generous personality as well as her flashing temper as a child.

with characteristic energy. "Your daughter," the French tutor, Mlle. Gremaux, told Marie, "has a will of iron. She is determined to get what she wants." The information did not surprise her mother.

Marie frequently visited friends at the Dijon garrison and, during summer months, toured various French military installations with her daughters. Elizabeth thrilled to the bustle, parades, sham cavalry fights, and military bands.

Her mother and her tutors combined to help Elizabeth develop a certain poise and gradually to cap her volcanic temper. Before she reached her teens, her piano artistry won considerable admiration among Dijon critics. Once, following a performance that brought the audience to its feet, she walked offstage to her waiting mother. "Well, how did I play my piece?" she inquired, her black eyes boring into her mother. Marie, determined not to add conceit to her daughter's already volatile personality, responded, "Fairly well," and awaited the explosion. Much to Marie's surprise, Elizabeth calmly responded, "I shall try harder another time."

Marie Catez, forty-four, poses with her daughters at their Dijon home three years after Joseph's death.

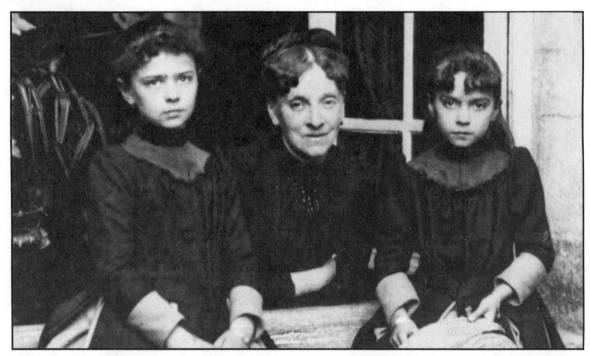

*   *   *   *   *

Marie's years of struggle to bridle her daughter's temper were bearing fruit. The intervals between tantrums grew longer and longer.

Elizabeth's playmates accepted her as a natural leader. "She shed a lively influence all around her," a friend recollected. The same friend added: "She was quickly roused, but I cannot count the times I saw her biting her lip so as not to answer back when reproved or to repress a nasty remark."

Another factor, in addition to Marie's unrelenting discipline, contributed to the gradual calming of Elizabeth's tempestuous spirit. From the time she was seven, Elizabeth evidenced an unusually deep religious bent. She prayed with the same fervor that characterized everything she did. At prayer, she presented an image of tranquility and concentration.

While preparing for first communion at the age of ten, she had little difficulty discovering her major fault. Indeed, she did penance even before her first confession. On one occasion, the priest instructing her class sentenced Elizabeth and a little friend to kneel on the walk outside the church. History hides details of their heinous crime. The episode, however, reveals that, although Elizabeth had not yet achieved perfection, she had made some gains. No record exists of her kicking the pews or yelling out, "Bad priest!" when sentenced.

During her first communion Mass and thanksgiving, tears of joy trickled down her face. She told her friend, "I am

Elizabeth made her first communion at the age of ten. Already she had manifested a deeply religious nature, as well as an attraction to the local Carmelite monastery.

not hungry . . . Jesus has fed me." The evening after receiving her first communion, Elizabeth persuaded her mother to visit the Carmelite monastery near their home in Dijon. The prioress, Mother Marie of Jesus, told the first communicant her name meant "the House of God," gave her a holy picture, and inscribed "Elizabeth" on the back. Beneath the name was this little poem:

Thy blessed name, O child, a
　mystery hides.
On this great day revealed.
God who is Love, within thy
　heart abides,
His temple here below.

*　　*　　*　　*　　*

A Dijon newspaper reported in August, 1893, "Mlle. Catez, first prize at the piano of M. Dietrich's class, received unanimous applause after the *Capriccio Brilliant* of Mendelssohn. It was a pleasure to see this young child scarcely thirteen years old come to the piano; she is already a distinguished pianist with an excellent touch, a beautiful tone, and a real musical feeling. A debut like this permits us to base great hopes on this child."

At thirteen, Elizabeth won first prize as a pianist at the Dijon Conservatory and was highly praised by local music critics for her brilliant musical skill.

But all was not first prizes and warm applause for Elizabeth, nor had she yet reached perfection. In a letter of 1894, she related how the prize of excellence in a major piano competition was unjustly snatched from her.

The same year, 1894, Mlle. Forey, her French tutor, asked Elizabeth to write a self-portrait.

> To draw one's physical and moral portrait is a delicate subject to deal with, [she wrote] but, taking my courage in both hands, I set to work and begin!
>
> Without pride, I think I can say that my overall appearance is not displeasing. I am a brunette and, they say, rather tall for my age. I have sparkling black eyes and thick eyebrows give me a severe look. The rest of my person is insignificant. My "dainty" feet could win for me the nickname "Elizabeth of the Big Feet," like Queen Bertha! And there you have my physical portrait!
>
> As for my moral portrait, I would say that I have a rather good character. I am cheerful and, I must confess, somewhat scatterbrained. I have a good heart. I am by nature a coquette. "One should be little!" they say. I am not lazy: I know "work makes us happy." Without being a model of patience, I usually know how to control myself. I do not hold grudges. So much for my moral portrait. I have my defects and, alas, few good qualities! I hope to acquire them!
>
> Well, at last this tedious task is finished, and am I glad!

Dijon music critics continued to follow Elizabeth's progress with growing enthusiasm. "No one can interpret the great masters as she does," one exclaimed. "Elizabeth has the soul for it."

Few who knew the vivacious, charming, and coquettish Mlle. Catez would believe what her diary revealed at this stage. "I was very fond of prayer and I loved God so much" she wrote, "that, even before my first communion, I could not understand how it was possible to give one's heart to anyone else. From that time, I was determined to love him alone and to live only for him. At fourteen, I bound myself to him by a vow of virginity."

At the time she made her private vow, she also determined to enter the Carmelite monastery in Dijon. When her mother suspected this decision, she forbade Elizabeth to visit the Carmelite cloister. Elizabeth obeyed.

The public entrance to the chapel of the Carmelite community: Marie Catez forbade her daughter to visit the monastery during her teen years, hoping to dissuade her from entering the cloister.

The main altar of the Dijon Carmelite monastery.

Father Isidore Angles, pastor of Carcassone, an old family friend, corresponded regularly with Elizabeth. "She was holy from her early years," the priest testified. "She was lively, ardent, and passionate. Born in a camp, she felt the soldier's blood, hot and generous, coursing through her veins. Two loves kept her fiery, hot-headed, self-willed nature under control — the love of her mother and the love of God."

Her decision to join the Carmelites was no surprise to the priest. Indeed, she had told him of her desire when she was only seven years of age. "How silly," retorted Madame Catez when Father Angles told her about Elizabeth's early desires.

Her diary contains a poem she wrote about this time.

Jesus, my soul desires you;
I want to be your bride soon.
With you I want to suffer
And, to find you, die.

Elizabeth showed the poem to neither Mlle. Forey nor her mother. Mlle. Forey would never have understood; her mother would never have approved.

Every moment of Elizabeth's day became for her an opportunity to unite herself with the suffering Christ. She elaborated what she called the "Clock of the Passion." Each time she awoke during the night hours, she joined her heart with that of Christ suffering during the long night before his death. During the day, she offered every little pain or inconvenience to Jesus. Her "Clock of the Passion" wound through twenty-four hours and marked her efforts to control her temper. "We should never let an hour go by without making a sacrifice," she wrote in her diary. "I had the joy of offering Jesus today several sacrifices with respect to my dominant fault, but how much they cost me! When I am unjustly reproved, I feel as though the blood is boiling in my veins. My whole being rises in revolt, but I hear my Lord's voice down deep in my heart. Then I am ready to bear everything for the love of him."

The clock beat steadily as she struggled to express her love for the crucified Savior in her dealings with others. "I never heard her speak ill of anybody," a friend remembered. "She could do justice to the good in each one, yet without denying their failings; her tact equaled her charity just as her indulgence did not hinder her from being firm when necessary."

Elizabeth manifested a tenderness that must have been most difficult for her competitive nature. She wrote of a fellow pianist, frightened before a recital: "I shall pray that God may take possession of Madeleine, even to the tips of her little fingers; then I challenge anyone to rival her. Do not let her feel nervous. I will tell her my secret: she must forget all those who are listening to her and imagine that she is alone with the Divine Master. Then one plays for him with one's whole soul and the piano gives out its notes full and strong, and yet sweet."

As Elizabeth matured, her mother grasped at every straw that might indicate a weakening of her determination to become a Carmelite nun. Hoping against hope that some young officer might turn her head, she encouraged Elizabeth to enjoy the active social life of the military personnel at Dijon. Each summer, accompanied by her two daughters, Marie visited friends and relatives at various military installations. During these excursions, Elizabeth attended a constant round of parties. She enjoyed them all. "Elizabeth appeared," a friend related, "irreproachably dressed, simply but elegantly, without anything overstudied or pretentious. Good taste guided her in her dress as in everything else. To see her thus, winsome and gracious, no one would have thought she was longing only to enter the religious life."

Marie, sensing that her efforts to change Elizabeth's mind were doomed, poured out her frustrations on the younger Marguerite.

"Elizabeth is praying all the time to enter the cloister, Mother," Marguerite told her anguished mother.

"When mother realized my intention was unchanged," Elizabeth recorded in her diary, "she cried very much and told me she would not hinder my going when I was twenty-one." Elizabeth added: "Dear Lord, support her. Her grief is painful to see."

Elizabeth and Marguerite posed together for this photo in the spring of 1901 just before Elizabeth left for the cloister.

Marie fell seriously ill. Elizabeth, anxious and fretful, got up in the night to listen to her mother's breathing. Fearing for her life, she prayed to God to cure the illness. Her mother improved. "At last, mother has recovered," Elizabeth wrote in her diary. "O my good Master, what a trial you sent me in this."

*   *   *   *   *

As the nineteenth century closed, the Redemptorists conducted a parish mission in Dijon. "How much I admire them," Elizabeth wrote. "They have been able to follow their vocation and have the happiness of bringing back many souls to God. Lord, when shall I be able to follow my vocation? When shall I be able to give myself to you?"

Marie, not yet reconciled to Elizabeth's desire to enter religious life, made one last-ditch effort to change her mind.

"This morning," Elizabeth wrote, "mother returned home very late and very upset. She had been approached with a marriage proposal for me, a brilliant match such as I shall never have the chance of making again. So she went to ask advice of my confessor. He required her to tell me of this proposal and point out its advantages, saying that it is a test for me; that I must think about it. I was far from expecting this, but how indifferent I am to this attractive project. My heart is not free. I have given it to the King of Kings and I can no longer dispose of it. Mother is wonderful. She is not even trying to rouse my emotions. When she asked me to consider the matter, I told her that my answer would be the same a week hence as today. Now she understands me."

Marie told Elizabeth: "It would have been a comfort to me but, since God wills otherwise, may his will be done."

She gave nineteen-year-old Elizabeth permission to resume her visits to the Carmelite convent. "What an entrancing child she is," the mother prioress wrote of Elizabeth. "Her visits always refresh me."

During the two years preceding her entrance into Carmel, Elizabeth sought guidance from a Dominican priest, Father Irenee Vallee. He, recognizing the girl's unique spirit, provided theological underpinning for her religious experiences. "It was a real joy," he wrote, "to talk about the Lord and his grace with one so pure, so intuitive and also so simple; whose will, as also her understanding, had been given to God from the very beginning."

Starting with the words of St. Paul — "Do you not know that you are the temple of God and that the Spirit of God dwells within you?" — the Dominican demonstrated to Elizabeth how the Father, Son, and Holy Spirit make their abode within the human heart. He helped her understand her profound relationship with the three Divine Persons. Father Vallee's direction comforted her and encouraged her to develop a profound devotion to the blessed Trinity. At his suggestion, Elizabeth, who had hoped to receive the name "Elizabeth of Jesus" upon entering the convent, requested the name "Sister Elizabeth of the Blessed Trinity."

Mother prioress assessed Elizabeth from her own perspective. "For Elizabeth," she wrote, "love meant devoting herself, sacrificing herself, immolating herself. She felt a need to suffer and she longed for death. Contemplation alone would not satisfy her. She had to give herself. And how did she do that? She consecrated her life to God in the cloister and, drop by drop, she gave her blood.

She crucified her body, her heart and her soul until death."

For Elizabeth, her Carmelite vocation provided an opportunity to model herself completely after Christ, especially in his sufferings for the salvation of humanity. "I hope I shall suffer," she told the mother prioress. "I am going to Carmel only for that; and, if God were to spare me one single day of suffering, I would be afraid he had forgotten me."

She looked forward to death, for it would clear away the only obstacle preventing her embrace of God. "For me, death is as though a wall were to crumble, and I would fall into the arms of my Beloved," she wrote.

Dominican Father Irenee Vallee recognized Elizabeth's unique spirit and provided the theological underpinnings for her religious experiences by guiding her to a profound knowledge and love of scripture.

Shortly before Elizabeth entered the Dijon Carmel, Mother Marie of Jesus, the prioress, left Dijon to open a new monastery in Paray-le-Monial, a nearby city. Mother Marie planned to invite Elizabeth to join in the new venture. She ordered the nun making her postulant's habit to ship it to the new convent.

Elizabeth, realizing the move would create hardship for her mother and sister, received this news with some dismay. Her mother visited the mother prioress. Afterwards, the prioress wrote Elizabeth: "You doubtlessly know that your mother and your sister, Marguerite, have asked me to leave you at Dijon. It seems, moreover, that such is also your own wish. In all that, I see the will of the good God, which we must love and carry out without hesitation. I am receiving you for Dijon, my dear child."

Elizabeth received word that the nuns would welcome her to the Dijon cloister on August 2, 1901. The night before she left home for the convent, her mother, unable to sleep, came and knelt beside her bed. "We are both broken-hearted," her mother sobbed. "Why are you leaving?"

"O Mother dear, can I resist God's voice when he is calling me?" Elizabeth responded through tears. "He is stretching out his arms and telling me how he is ignored, outraged, forsaken. Can I also go away? He calls for victims. I must go, notwithstanding my grief at leaving you and plunging you into this sorrow. I must answer his call."

The next morning, when the moment came to leave home forever, Elizabeth knelt before her father's portrait and asked his blessing. Then, accompanied by her mother, Marguerite, and several girl friends, she went to the Carmelite

Mother Marie of Jesus, prioress of the Dijon Carmel when Elizabeth was growing up, encouraged the young girl to enter the cloister.

chapel. After Mass and communion, Marie took her daughter to the door of the cloister. As the door closed, Elizabeth cast a long last look at those she so fondly cherished.

"I love my mother as I never did before," she wrote Father Angles, "and, now that the time has come to consummate the sacrifice which will separate me from my dear mother and sister, what peace is flooding my soul! Already, I seem no longer on earth. I feel that I am all his and that I am keeping back nothing. I am throwing myself into his arms like a little child."

Like a bird singing on a spring morning, a fish swimming through a cool brook, a baby at play in a crib, Elizabeth, alive with joy, had found her environment. Her writings, cheerful and spontaneous, reveal an unearthly sense of peace, no matter what the subject.

She described her wash day:

I tucked up my dress for the occasion, donned a large apron and a pair of clogs to complete my costume, and went down to the laundry. Everyone was rubbing away with all her might, and I tried to do like the others. I splashed and soaked myself fairly well, but that mattered little; I was delighted. You know everything is delightful at Carmel, and we find God at the wash as at prayer. Everywhere there is only he; one breathes and lives in him.... If you knew how happy I am! My outlook widens every day.

To a friend, she wrote: "They take good care of me here at Carmel. I sleep soundly on a straw mattress. I did not feel very safe the first night; I thought I might roll off on one side or the other.

The door of the Carmelite cloister: At twenty-one, Elizabeth finally fulfilled her dream, saying to a tearful Marie, "Mother dear, can I resist God's voice when he is calling me?"

Nothing of the kind happened and now I am used to it. If you knew how I like everything at Carmel! The time passes quickly, and I feel as though I had always lived in this dear monastery."

She corresponded regularly with her mother and sister. The two visited the Dijon Carmel when allowed. Although the cloister grille separated them, the three women could see and speak with each other.

Elizabeth tried to console her mother by describing her deep happiness: "If you could but see my happiness, you would be bound to rejoice, for your permission was required before I could enter this corner of heaven. Thank you again, Mother, for having given it so bravely. If you knew how the good God loves you and how your daughter is more devoted to you than ever!"

Her first months at Carmel were filled with sweetness and delight. "You asked me what I do," she wrote a friend." A Carmelite has only to do two things — to love and to pray."

On December 8, 1901, Elizabeth was received into the novitiate and clothed in the Carmelite habit. As her novitiate progressed, she entered into the "dark night" which St. John of the Cross, the great Carmelite spiritual master, so

On the feast of the Immaculate Conception, 1901, Elizabeth, dressed in a white satin bridal gown, was received into the novitiate and clothed in the Carmelite habit.

vividly described. Anxieties, spiritual distress, strange imaginations crowded her heart. Candidly, she revealed her interior difficulties to Mother Germaine, the new prioress. "You must be patient," she was told; "God is asking you to trust him as a child trusts his father."

Father Vallee, aware of her suffering, returned again and again to the theme expressed in St. John's gospel: "God first loved us. His love is not like our imperfect love. We must return, as best we can, his perfect love to him. We must love him with his own love."

The fruit of her pain, the hard-won knowledge that God first loves us, enabled her to write to another Carmelite nun undergoing a similar deprivation: "During these painful times, when you feel a terrible void, think how God is enlarging the capacity of your soul so that it can receive him — making it, as it were, infinite as he is infinite. Look upon each pain as a love token coming to you directly from God in order to unite you to him."

Later, she wrote: "Think of this God who is dwelling within you, whose temple you are; little by little, the soul becomes accustomed to living in his gentle company; it understands how it bears within itself a little heaven, wherein the God of love has set his dwelling place. Then, as it were, the soul breathes in a divine atmosphere; I will even say that only the body remains on earth while the soul lives beyond the veil in him who is unchangeable. It is not by looking at our own miseries that we shall be cleansed, but by looking upon him who is all purity and all sanctity."

"When things are at their worst," she continued, "think how, in order to render his work more beautiful, the Divine Artist is using the chisel. Remain in peace beneath the hand that is working upon you. After having been taken to the third heaven, St. Paul felt his weakness and complained to God who answered him, 'My grace is sufficient for thee.' So, take courage."

*   *   *   *   *

After her two-year novitiate and passage through the "dark night," calm returned to Elizabeth's spirit and she made her profession of first vows on January 11, 1903.

After profession, she experienced no spiritual sweetness, but a deep peace flooded her being. "Who could describe my joy," she wrote in 1903, "when I look at the crucifix given me at my profession and placed by our mother prioress as a seal upon my heart? I could say to myself, 'At last, he is all mine and I am all his.' Now I have only one desire: to love him every moment like a true spouse; to be zealous for his honor, to make him happy by making a home for him, a shelter in my heart, there by my love to make him forget all the abominations committed by the wicked."

Later on, she wrote: "In order to reach the ideal life of the soul, I believe we must live in the supernatural, be persuaded that God dwells in our innermost being, and go to everything with him. Then, nothing can be trivial, no matter how commonplace in itself, for we do not live in those things but soar above them."

Shortly after profession, during a discussion with sister Carmelites concerning the passage in the book of Revelation that describes God as giving each of the elect a new name, Elizabeth declared, "Mine will be 'Praise of Glory.'" She cited St. Paul, whose writings provided the scriptural foundation of her spiritual life: "We have been predestined according to the purpose of him who works all things according to the counsel of his will, that we may become the praise of his glory."

She wrote to Marguerite about the discussion and raised the questions: "How can we realize this great dream of the heart of God, which is his unchanging plan for our souls? How are we to respond to our vocation which challenges us to become a perfect praise of glory to the Blessed Trinity?"

As she answered her own questions, she revealed the depths of her experience. "A 'Praise of Glory' is a soul that dwells in God, loves him with a love that is pure and disinterested, without seeking itself in the sweetness of this love; this soul must surrender itself completely, blindly, to God's will, so that it cannot possibly will anything but what God wills."

"A 'Praise of Glory,'" she continued, "is a silent soul, which remains like a lyre beneath the mysterious touch of the Holy Spirit. This soul knows that the string of suffering sounds more sweetly still, and therefore loves to have that string so that it may be more pleasing to the heart of God."

"A 'Praise of Glory,'" she added, "is a soul that gazes steadfastly upon God in faith and simplicity. It reflects all that he is; it is like a fathomless abyss into which he may flow and overflow."

"Lastly, a 'Praise of Glory,'" she concluded, "is a being ever in an attitude of thanksgiving; every one of its acts, its movements, thoughts, aspirations, while more deeply rooting it in love, is an echo of the eternal 'Holy, Holy, Holy Lord God Almighty.'"

Convinced that "the Praise of Glory of the Holy Trinity" begins on earth, in the heaven of our hearts, Elizabeth looked forward to death that would tear down the veil separating her from the infinite love of God.

Such sublime theology would have meant little unless it shaped Elizabeth's daily life. According to the testimony of sister Carmelites, Elizabeth — quiet, undemonstrative, cheerful — brought joy to their lives. She undertook the humblest tasks. She was the assistant portress. She worked in the sacristy. She did exquisite needlepoint and embroidery, and made habits for the Sisters. The hot-tempered little girl had matured into a gentle, unselfish, affectionate woman. "On several occasions when she found me in tears," a candidate wrote, "she took me in her arms affectionately and helped me to talk out my troubles with the prioress. She always treated me with reverence."

"She shed peace around her," a Carmelite nun recalled. "She showed such tact and simplicity and cordiality that she won everyone's confidence." Visitors who only met her at the cloister grille remembered: "It was impossible to come near her without being influenced, penetrated with the Presence of God.... Something of the grace that was in her seemed to pass through the grille that separated us."

After a visit, a friend wrote to Elizabeth's mother: "The love of God seemed to enfold her, yet she spoke so affectionately to me and talked of you with such an outburst of devotion that I cried then, as I cry now, when I recall the all-too-brief time I spent with her."

On her first anniversary at Carmel, Elizabeth wrote her mother: "It is a year ago that I gave to God the best of mothers, yet the great sacrifice has not separated our souls. Do you not feel that today we are more closely united than ever? Oh, let me tell you how divinely happy I am! My whole soul is overflowing to God and to you with gratitude."

To her sister, Marguerite, about to marry, she wrote: "Only God knows what I sacrificed in leaving you; and, if his love had not sustained us, I feel sure I could not have done it."

When Marguerite and her husband had their first child, whom they named Elizabeth, the cloistered nun wrote: "I feel filled with reverence before this small temple of the Holy Trinity. Her soul seems to me like a crystal reflecting God;

In December, 1902, Elizabeth, wearing a novice's white veil, enjoyed a rare visit with her mother (left) and Marguerite.

and, if I were beside her, I should go on my knees to adore him who is dwelling there."

Then she wrote to her mother: "Dear Grandmother. You have given God one Elizabeth and now he sends you another; we shall rival each other as to which will love you the more."

* * * * *

In the summer of 1903, doctors diagnosed Elizabeth as a victim of Addison's disease. At the time, there was no known cure for the ailment, which produces depression, irritability, and anemia, and often darkens the skin. For two years, despite her condition, Elizabeth carried on her daily routine of prayer and

work. By the spring of 1905, Mother Germaine exempted her from the rules of daily fasting. The prioress also relieved her of portress duties.

"How painful it was to me to be given exceptions. I felt such a need to follow my Master in his immolation," Elizabeth complained. When mother prioress permitted her to take the simple meal of the lenten fast throughout the penitential season, instead of the full meal ordered by the doctors, she noted cheerfully in her diary: "Never did an epicure experience at the sight of a sumptuous banquet what I felt that first evening of Lent at the sight of that frugal meal!"

Elizabeth informed her mother of her illness but never explained its seriousness. "Our kind prioress is looking after me in a real, motherly fashion," she wrote. "She is anxious for me to be out of doors. So, instead of working in my little cell, I am installed like a hermit in the garden and spend such happy hours there. To me, nature seems filled with God; the wind sighing in the tall trees, the little birds singing, the lovely blue sky; everything speaks of him. O Mother, I feel I must tell how my happiness continues to increase; it is taking

In the cloister garden, Elizabeth spoke to Christ of her love in unmistakable terms: "I long to be the bride of your heart . . . and love you until I die of love!"

on infinite proportions, like God himself, and it is such calm, sweet happiness!"

In the fall of 1905 after a retreat, she wrote: "God has given me such light upon our holy vocation. He shows it to me as so high and so sublime that I beg him not to let me live long. Cowardly as I am, it seems to me so difficult to reach this standard and to maintain it. He has many means of supplying for the glory he might expect from his humble 'Praise of Glory' here below. He can make me fulfill a long space in a few days. He knows how I love him and want to suffer for him."

That Christmas, while Elizabeth was arranging the crib, a nun overheard her say to the Infant Jesus: "Well, my little King of Love, next year we shall see each other at closer quarters."

As the year 1906 opened, the disease began its final occupation of her body: "I could not find a comfortable position, nor could I sleep soundly," she wrote. "As regards exhaustion, I cannot say whether the night or the day is worse." Elizabeth, at last, had reached her Calvary. She longed for these sacrifices. She was discovering how true were her own words: "There are exchanges of love that take place only on the cross."

At the end of March, 1906, mother prioress ordered her into the convent infirmary. "I have no duty," Elizabeth wrote, "except that of loving."

She offered her frequent, violent pain for France, then careening through a periodic course of persecution of the Roman Catholic church. Premier Justin Emile Combes, who had spent his youth studying for the priesthood and had left the seminary just before ordination, directed the anti-Catholic drive. Before his resignation from office in 1905, the feckless Combes disrupted Vatican-French relations, forced priests and nuns into exile and drove cloistered nuns and monks out of their monasteries. The Carmelite convent at Dijon escaped the scourge but nevertheless lived in fear of the government's heavy and capricious hand. "Poor France," Elizabeth wrote, "I long to cover her with the blood of the Just One and to beg for mercy."

Elizabeth had never told her mother about the progress of the disease. When Marie discovered that the prioress had transferred her to the infirmary, she suffered the deepest distress. Because cloister rules did not allow her to enter the infirmary, she could only imagine her daughter's condition. To her anxious letter, Elizabeth replied: "Dear Mother, never did I feel so near you; your letter rejoiced me and was a rest for my soul." Elizabeth then noted her unhappiness at surviving the latest onslaught of her illness. "Had I departed for heaven, how I would have lived with you. I would never have left you and I would have made you feel the presence of your little Elizabeth."

As the pain mounted, Elizabeth experienced a new intensity of contemplation and union with God. "Oh," she wrote, "I have never been so happy as since God deigned to associate me to the sufferings of the Divine Master. I go with Christ to my passion in order to participate in his work of redemption." To her mother, she wrote, "God has sealed me with the cross of his Son."

She prayed to Therese of Lisieux, the young Carmelite nun who had died eight years earlier, seeking her intercession for the restoration of her ability to walk. Her prayers were answered to the extent that she was able to take a daily walk on the convent terrace with the assistance of the mother prioress. "I look like a little old lady bent over my stick," she wrote to her mother.

Sometimes Elizabeth stumbled alone to a balcony attached to the infirmary that overlooked the chapel. "How often when I passed by the tribune," one nun remembered, "I cast a glance into it. It seemed empty. It was necessary to go very near in order to see, right at the end of it, our dear Sister Elizabeth, huddled up on the floor in a little dark corner. She looked to me like the personification of prayer and pain.

She wrote to Father Vallee on August 2: "Do you remember? Five years ago today, I knocked at the door of Carmel and you were there to bless my first steps into the desert. Now it is at the eternal gates I am knocking." Then she wrote her mother: "Do you remember five years ago? Jesus caught the blood of your mother's heart in a chalice which will weigh very heavily on the scales of his mercy."

As the summer passed and the disease burned out of control, Elizabeth's spirits soared. She kept notes during sleepless nights and entitled them, "Notes from the Palace of Pain and Happiness."

"Your little 'Praise of Glory' cannot sleep," she wrote God. "She is in pain, but, despite the agony, her soul is peaceful." To a friend, she wrote, "I feel ready to go through fire to do more perfectly anything God wills."

As fall began, she wrote: "I have a continual pain about my heart and I am beginning to lose my sense of smell. My dreadful mouth can no longer even taste."

At September's end, she insisted on making the white veil for a lay sister postulant who was soon to receive the Carmelite habit. "No one who watched her skill, the good taste with which she arranged everything, as also her forethought with which she provided for the smallest details," a Carmelite recalled, "would have thought that the following week she would take to her bed, never to rise from it again."

Elizabeth united her heart completely to that of the suffering Christ. "Yesterday evening," she told the prioress, "my soul was powerless. All at once I felt overwhelmed with love. It was like fire, yet infinitely sweet; at the same time, it seemed to deal me a mortal wound."

St. John of the Cross, her Carmelite mentor, wrote two centuries earlier about mystics like her: "They die amid delectable encounters and impulses of love, like the swan which sings most sweetly when it is at the point of death."

Elizabeth, her stomach almost entirely destroyed, could hardly tolerate even a few drops of barley sugar. On the feast of All Saints, she received her last communion on earth, a tiny fragment of the host. To counter her violent headaches, the nuns applied ice which her intense fever melted almost at once. Her eyes, bloodshot, closed. She did not reopen them until November 9, 1906, during her last hour.

Despite Elizabeth's excruciating pain, a Carmelite nun related: "To watch by her bedside was consoling rather than fatiguing. So strongly did I feel our Lord's presence in her that I used to kiss her hands with the same reverence and faith as I would have kissed those of Jesus crucified. I shall not forget the last

Mother Germaine of Jesus, Elizabeth's prioress at Dijon and her first biographer, had a deep affection for Elizabeth and a profound admiration for the young nun's holiness.

moments before her blessed death. She still seemed to speak St. Paul's language: 'I have fought the good fight, I have finished the race. From now on a merited crown awaits me.'"

During her last illness, Elizabeth often referred to her prioress as her priest, in the sense that, for Elizabeth, the will of Mother Germaine represented the will of God. She had written a little poem for the prioress; its words sum up her life.

> "Where shall we find the Master?" wrote a saint.
> "Where is his house, save in the midst of pain."
> There would I dwell, my mother and my priest,
> To magnify the Cross where he was slain.
> But yet I need thee, 'neath thy sheltering wing,
> To enter this fair palace of my Lord,
> This fortress, the strong citadel of God,
> Which to the soul doth changeless peace afford.
> David hath sung: "Christ's sorrow is immense!"
> In this immensity my home I make;
> In sacred silence, self I immolate,
> Transformed into love's victim for his sake.

Sister Elizabeth of the Trinity was beatified November 25, 1984. Her feast is celebrated on November 8.

*   *   *   *   *

Marie Catez lived for eight years after her daughter's death. She died March 10, 1914, after long months of illness.

Difficult as it was for her, Marie gradually accepted the death of her daughter in a spirit of faith. "Earnest and sensitive," one of Elizabeth's biographers wrote of Marie, "she became ever more established in peace and abandonment to the will of God, and her perfect conformity to that will moved the hearts of those around her."

Elizabeth, during her own last days, had written her mother: "I have sacrificed all on the altar in my heart to Christ. To say that it cost me nothing would be far indeed from the truth. Sometimes I ask myself how I could have left so good a mother, but the more we give to God the more he gives himself also."

Pauline Jaricot

"Your Holiness, Mademoiselle Jaricot, the Frenchwoman whom you wished to see this week, is too ill to keep her appointment." Cardinal Lambruschini, the papal secretary of state, barely concealed his disappointment as he advised Pope Gregory XVI of the unhappy turn of events. The pope had been looking forward for some time that summer of 1835 to a meeting with Mademoiselle Jaricot. The thirty-five-year-old Pauline had wrought wonders for Catholicism in her native land where the church was still reeling from blows suffered during the French Revolution.

"What is wrong with Mademoiselle Jaricot?" the pope asked.

"She has a chronic heart condition, Your Holiness, and recently underwent lung surgery. She is a woman of strong character, however, and insisted on making the journey to Rome."

"Where is she now?"

"She is at Mere Madeleine Sophie Barat's Convent of the Sacred Heart."

"Well, if Mademoiselle Jaricot cannot come to the pope, the pope will have to come to her. Advise Mere Barat of our visit and arrange a time."

*　　*　　*　　*　　*

Endowed with keen business sense, Pauline's father Antoine, a wealthy merchant in Lyons, was, above all, a man of faith and integrity.

Pauline's mother Jeanne died while devotedly but frantically nursing her daughter after a tragic fall.

Pauline inherited her strong character from her parents, Antoine and Jeanne. Her father, the thirteenth child of a poor shepherd, arrived in Lyons as an orphan at fourteen years of age. Young Antoine, through intelligence, wit, courage, and hard work, survived poverty, siege, and a price on his head to emerge from the Revolution as one of the leading silk merchants of Lyons. As the bloody wave of violence and disorder receded, Lyons lay ravaged and exhausted. Antoine devoted himself to leading the ancient and once elegant city to new prosperity and prestige.

Pauline, the seventh child of Antoine Jaricot and Jeanne Lattier, was born July 22, 1799. The family baby, she was Daddy's favorite, Mama's joy, and the center of all attention — especially that of her brother Phileas, two years her senior. From childhood, he frequently informed the family that he planned to become a missionary to China. "Take me with you, Phileas," his younger sister would plead.

"No, little one," Phileas would counter, "you must stay home and raise barrels of money so I can rescue Chinese babies for baptism."

Pauline made her first communion in 1812. As she entered her midteens, she possessed charm, style, extraordinary beauty, and wealth. Contemporaries described her as slightly above medium height, with a slender figure and at times a coquettish manner. Long, dark curls framed her oval face. Her eyes, dark brown, snapped with intelligence and humor. She was an excellent dancer who sometimes wore through the soles of her dainty dancing slippers at an evening's ball. The object of male attention and female envy, Pauline wrote: "I would have had to be made of ice not to enjoy the flattery, compliments, and gentle words of praise I received."

In 1814 when the city of Lyons, celebrating the Bourbon return to the French throne, tendered an official reception to the Duchess of Angouleme, city officials appointed Pauline a lady-in-waiting to the duchess. Pauline, vain and frivolous, was delighted over her role in the whole affair, and especially in the knowledge that her fiancé's social position entitled him to an invitation to the great event. She and the young man had secretly engaged themselves to be married. Pauline wore a pendant about her slender throat as a symbol of their love.

*   *   *   *   *

Pauline (left) and her sister Sophie. Although children of the rich, they learned from their parents early in life to respect workers and to love the poor.

Pauline loved Lyons, the place of her birth, her labors, her successes, and her defeats.

Three months after her triumph at the ball in honor of the duchess, the blooming beauty lay in bed, a limp and wasted flower. The brown eyes had lost their luster, the white skin its glow. A home accident, followed by inept medical treatment, unleashed the melancholy.

In October, 1814, Pauline, stretching for a box on top of her wardrobe, fell to the floor from the stool on which she was standing. Her doctor, unable to find any broken bones, decided to bleed her, a common medical procedure of the time. The bleeding caused anemia and her physical system deteriorated. She grew thin and pale, suffered convulsions, and lost her power of speech. She experienced severe chest pains and body spasms. The once graceful dancer moved only in spastic jerks. The physical suffering caused her great pain, but another fear terrorized her more. She was afraid of losing her mind. "O God," she prayed, "take my life rather than my reason."

She sent word to her fiancé that she did not wish to see him. The family doctor ordered the invalid to Tassin, the Jaricot country home outside of Lyons. Pauline's mother, Jeanne, insisting on nursing her daughter herself, pursued her duties so frantically that she also took ill and died within several weeks.

Antoine, fearful that the news of her mother's death might snap the few thin threads binding Pauline to the real world, ordered no one to tell her of it. When anyone, servant or family, visited her at Tassin, they wore no signs of mourning. The full household was sorely tried, fabricating excuses why Jeanne did not visit Pauline and no longer nursed her.

One day the parish priest of Tassin visited Pauline and suggested that she receive communion. After much hesitation, the girl agreed. "And confession, Mademoiselle?" the priest inquired. "No, Father, no!" the terrified girl replied. The priest spoke gently to her. Finally she decided to make her confession. Then she received holy communion.

The two sacraments initiated a slow healing process. Pauline gradually regained control of her mind and body. Eight months after the doctors sent her to Tassin, she returned to Lyons. Her father, worried lest she suffer further sorrow on returning to her former home with all of its memories of her mother, purchased a new home for his favorite daughter.

Pauline once more entered the social whirl of Lyons. Again she commanded attention for her creative dress, coquetting, and superb style. After a night of dance, however, she would return home, throw herself on her bed, and burst into tears. "What is wrong with me?" she would lament to her maid and her confessor, her only confidants. "You are only grieving for your mother, Pauline," they both assured her.

One Sunday in Lent, 1816, Pauline attended a Mass celebrated by Father Wendel Wurtz, an outspoken and courageous priest. Ordained on the eve of the French Revolution, he had fled to Italy as an exile rather than take the civil oath demanded by the revolutionary government. After Napoleon restored order to France, he returned to his native land.

In his homily that fateful Sunday morning, the priest leveled a blistering attack on vanity, a vice prevalent among many wealthy Catholics of Lyons. Pauline, stunning as usual in a pale blue silk dress, blue silk shoes, and leghorn hat trimmed with roses, judged the preacher was taking direct aim at her. After the Mass she went to the sacristy. "Father, what do you mean by this *sin* of vanity?"

"For some women it consists in adorning themselves so that they will be the idols of other humans," the priest answered. "For others," he continued, gazing steadily at the stylish young woman, "it consists in the love of what holds the heart captive when God is asking a person to rise to higher things."

"Will you take a few moments to hear my confession?" Pauline inquired. "Certainly, Mademoiselle," he responded.

From the time of that confession to the end of her life, Pauline acknowledged that she wanted to serve God, and him alone.

*   *   *   *   *

During the next year Pauline, with Father Wurtz's counsel, established her life's direction. She visited the most abandoned people and the contagiously ill, both in their poor homes and in Lyons' hospitals. She sold her jewelry and gave the money to the poor. She turned her beautiful dresses into vestments for the altar. She placed the gifts of her many male admirers at the foot of the crucifix in her room. She clothed herself in a plain, simple dress of a purple hue that she despised.

The Jaricot family was astounded. Her brother Paul, a practical businessman, expressed family reaction with a proverb. "Pauline, you are taking your soup too hot," he advised, "let it cool a bit."

The church of St.-Nizier was the most fashionable in Lyons. It was here that Pauline heard the sermon that prompted her religious conversion.

"I took such extreme measures because, if I had not broken off all at once," Pauline remarked, "I would not have done it at all. For the first several months, every time I met one of my girl friends dressed in the latest fashion I suffered bitterly."

These drastic measures freed Pauline to give her heart to God alone. She began to see and be aware of God everywhere — in the beauty of the trees and flowers, in every growing thing, and, above all, in the eyes of the poor. "The poor gave me the honor of receiving my alms," she said. "I saw the ravages of ignorance and poverty and vice amongst them; but, more than that, I saw Jesus in them. In serving them, I served the Lord."

At Christmas time, 1816, at the famous Marian shrine at Fourviere, Pauline knelt before the statue of the Blessed Mother and vowed perpetual chastity.

To help with the service of the poor, Pauline organized young women factory workers, and some wealthy young ladies as well, into a group she called

The poor suffered and died in the streets and alleys of Lyons' slums. "It is painful to see these members of our Lord suffering and to do nothing for them," wrote Pauline.

"The Penitents." She established a simple rule of life for them. They were to go wherever they felt they could best serve the poor. Pauline held meetings each week at her father's home for the Penitents. At the meetings, each young lady advised the group of a person or persons in need and described what she was doing to help. Although only eighteen years of age, Pauline already manifested a talent of leadership based on her genius for organization and her ability to inspire others.

At the root of all her activity lay a deep spirituality. A little book, *Infinite Love in the Divine Eucharist*, which she published anonymously in 1822, revealed the intensity of her relationship with Christ. Pauline became so closely united with Christ, whom she receive daily in holy communion, that he was the soul of her soul, the heart of her heart, with whom she experienced the daily joys and sufferings of life.

On the evening of Palm Sunday, 1817, while Pauline was kneeling before the tabernacle in prayer for the conversion of sinners and the salvation of her country, she suddenly became intensely aware of Christ's presence. "Will you suffer and die for me?" Christ asked her. Trembling with fear, she responded, "Yes."

"Then prepare to die, Pauline," Christ told her. He added: "If you remain faithful to your word, I will transform you into myself."

*   *   *   *   *

During the Revolution and its aftermath, overseas missionary activity, which had been the glory of French Catholicism, had practically ceased. But the French church, after being purged in the crucible of persecution, renewed and expanded its missionary effort. Although French priests and religious evangelized many nations, they directed their main efforts to two major areas, North America and the Orient. Before the Revolution, the French crown had generously provided funds for the missions. In post-revolutionary France, however, these resources were no longer available.

In 1818 the French Foreign Missionary Society organized lay people to assist the missions with their prayers and with whatever alms they could afford. Pauline joined this organization and recruited many of her girl friends as members. While on vacation that year, she visited a factory and asked each worker for a sou (equivalent then to a U.S. penny) to support the missions. The response of the poor workers was immediate and generous, and planted an idea in her mind that eventually revolutionized missionary fundraising.

It took about a year of prayer and reflection for Pauline to give clear and definite shape to that inspiration. Her plan envisioned a model organization of contributors and fund collectors that could be multiplied ad infinitum. The base level of the model would consist of ten contributors whose weekly offerings would be collected by a leader. The leader would pass the contributions (totaling ten sous) to a collector on a second level who would be in charge of ten base-level collectors (for a total of 100 sous). This amount would be passed along to a collector on a third level who would be in charge of ten second-level collectors (a total of 1,000 sous). The amount collected by the third-level collector would be turned over to a director for transfer to the central fund.

Pauline eagerly explained her plan to Father Wurtz. "Pauline, dearest," he responded, "you are not clever enough to have conceived anything like this. The plan must have come from God. So, go ahead and put it into operation." Father Wurtz was right. The plan immediately caught on in France. Within two years, the Propagation of the Faith, as the organization was called, donated four thousand dollars in support of the worldwide French missionary endeavor. The Propagation of the Faith subsequently became a worldwide organization contributing millions of dollars to the church's missions.

Despite its success, or perhaps because of it, Pauline became the target of criticism in the French church. Some bishops and clergy muttered and moaned at the spectacle of a mere girl sticking her nose into clerical business. Other missionary-collecting organizations, envious of her success, mounted opposition to the newly founded Propagation of the Faith.

Although harsh words and cruel judgments hurt and stung, Pauline did not halt her efforts. Two years after founding the Propagation of the Faith, she willingly surrendered its leadership to a board of directors composed of leading Catholic laymen of Lyons.

At the same time and in the same year, 1822, she started an artificial flower business which soon proved successful. All of its revenues were given to the poor.

The year 1822 was not all good. Pauline, worn out by hard work, worry, and storms of criticism, fell ill. "Her constitution is as spent as that of a person of seventy," the doctor advised her father. "She has a congested liver, an infected lung, and a bad heart." The doctor prepared Antoine to accept the fact that she would probably be an invalid for the rest of her life. Despite the doctor's glum predictions, however, she returned to her work within two weeks.

*   *   *   *   *

Indomitable Pauline, having made her singular contribution to mission fundraising, turned her attention to another element for successful evangelization — prayer. Using the organizational scheme that served the Propagation of the Faith so well, in 1826 she organized people in groups of fifteen, each of whom would pray a decade of the rosary daily. Thus, the group would collectively pray every day all the mysteries of the rosary. Each member contributed five francs a year for the purchase of Catholic books to counteract the atheistic and anti-Christian literature flooding France after the Revolution. Members of the Living Rosary, as Pauline called her new organization, dedicated their prayers to two purposes: that those who had never had the faith would receive it, and that those who had abandoned the faith would return to it. Pauline's prayer program, the fruit of her organizational ability, received generous response. Within ten years of its founding, more than two million French men and women united their hearts in the daily Living Rosary.

Those who had opposed Pauline's fundraising efforts took new scandal at the rosary promotion. Some clergy and some lay persons, ignoring the facts that her father consistently bankrolled her various apostolates and that she was independently wealthy, claimed she was using the money raised by the Living Rosary for her own purpose.

To validate her leadership, Pauline appealed to Pope Gregory XVI for approval of the Living Rosary and Good Book Society. The Pope issued a formal statement of approval and dispatched it to France. Clerical opponents intercepted the documents, however, and Pauline did not receive her papal credentials at that time.

*   *   *   *   *

Phileas, ordained in Paris in 1823, never realized his dream of becoming a missionary to China. His superiors judged his health too poor. So, Pauline's favorite brother returned to Lyons in 1825 and assumed the chaplaincy at the charity hospital there.

Religious sisters had formerly conducted the institution, but, because they refused to take an oath of allegiance to the revolutionary government, the state suppressed their community. Some of the nuns remained as employees, but they represented only a small percentage of the staff. Phileas, concerned for the sisters, rented a home for them on Lyons' Fourviere hillside. The property was called Nazareth. From its terraces, the sisters had a spectacular view of the winding rivers, gardens, cornfields, and pastures of the countryside around the city. On clear days the snowcapped peak of Mont Blanc back-lighted the magnificent setting. Phileas established a rule of life for the sisters and provided spiritual direction for them. As he carefully nurtured the little group back into organized religious life, other young women came to join the tiny Nazareth community. Soon the group had fifteen novices.

At the hospital, however, anti-religious authorities did not look kindly on Phileas' successful efforts to reorganize the sisters. When the priest discovered large-scale pilfering by employees of sheets, bandages, medicines, and food that benefactors had provided for the sick poor, he publicly complained of the thievery. Infuriated hospital workers poisoned his food. The priest suffered terribly but survived.

After a short rest the brave priest returned to his hospital duties and continued his campaign against stealing. "These goods belong to the poor," Phileas announced. "And our poor patients are at the mercy of cruel thieves.

Pauline's brother Phileas, a priest with a lifelong interest in the missions, encouraged her to initiate the fundraising effort that eventually became the worldwide Society of the Propagation of the Faith.

I must protest. If I do not protect the poor, who will?" His enemies made a second poisoning attempt, and this time succeeded. Phileas died in frightful pain. Pauline nursed him during his illness and final agony. "My brother," she lamented, "has done nothing but good for others. How could men treat him so cruelly?"

*   *   *   *   *

During Pauline's youth, two revolutions were occurring simultaneously in France. The French Revolution attempted to restore paganism. The Industrial Revolution was transferring the economic base of French wealth from agriculture to industry. The new rich industrialists, unfortunately, had little social conscious-ness and paid French factory workers very poorly. Farmers, attracted to city life, left their fields for factories. The cities, unable to accommodate the rapid influx, spawned slum areas. Laborers spent twelve to fourteen hours a day in the fac-tories and for this earned only a few sous. Vice, corruption, illness, and disease abounded as working families crowded into the slums of industrial cities. As the nineteenth century dawned, the Industrial Revolution slowly and thoroughly began to change French thought, culture, and civilization.

Government troops bombarded enemy barricades in Lyons during the Workers' Revolt of 1834.

The long-simmering unrest exploded in Lyons in November, 1831, when for two days and nights, thousands of workers roamed the city streets, refusing to enter the factories. Three thousand national guardsmen attempted to restore order. When enraged workers drove them from the city, National Guard General Roguet, shamed by his defeat, swore he would return and put Lyons to the torch. Pauline sent word to her Living Rosary members to pray for the deliverance of her beloved city. A few weeks later Roguet returned to the city with reinforcements. Along the route of the military, Rosarians had scattered little medals and handwritten messages praising the Blessed Mother. Some soldiers laughed at this simple gesture, but others read the messages and took the medals. When Roguet's forces occupied Lyons, some of the troops sought out the headquarters of the Living Rosary to ask for rosaries and scapulars. Pauline's prayer crusade and the reluctance of guardsmen to punish their fellow workers combined for a peaceful settlement of the revolt. General Roguet never fulfilled his vow.

*   *   *   *   *

In August, 1832, Pauline purchased a home on the hillside of Fourviere. She called it "Lorette" after the shrine of Our Lady of Loreto in Italy. Some of the religious sisters, formerly under Phileas' direction, and some working girls joined Pauline to form a loosely structured community at Lorette. She called the group the "Daughters of Mary." The members pursued a life of prayer and work for the salvation of sinners. Its informal organization enabled the community to respond quickly and concretely to individual needs of the poor. Father John Vianney, the famous Cure of Ars, made occasional visits to Lorette, leaving his village in the early morning hours to walk the nine miles to Lyons. Pauline contributed funds and clothing for his orphanage at Ars. She and the Cure shared a common devotion to Philomena, a popular cult "saint-figure" of the time.

*   *   *   *   *

In 1834 labor unrest in Lyons issued once more in civil strife. This time the workers were well armed and met government troops with fierce resistance. Firing from behind cobblestone barricades, tenement windows, and rooftops, the workers took a terrible toll on the government forces. The regular army rolled in artillery and bombarded the city. Fires blazed throughout Lyons, bridges were destroyed, factories collapsed, and homes burned to the ground.

At Lorette, Pauline and her community, caught in crossfire between government and labor forces, cowered under their beds. Bullets and shells tore through the walls, broke the house's stone facing, smashed the altar and pews. Shrapnel ricocheted around the rooms. Pauline, seriously ill, and her companions took shelter in a nearby cave that had in ancient times been a catacomb for the city's first Christians. Fighting continued for several days until the workers ran out of ammunition.

Casualties were heavy on both sides. Five hundred combatants died; hundreds more were wounded. Pauline and her little group returned to Lorette, determined to seek some peaceful means to right the social injustices that provided civil war, hatred, and slaughter. It took Pauline ten years to develop the beginnings of a practical solution to improve social conditions.

*   *   *   *   *

In December, 1834, Pauline's beloved father, Antoine, died. "His faith was wonderful," she told a friend. "It is dearer to me than titles of nobility."

Because critics of the Living Rosary still badgered her, Pauline decided to journey to Rome and request from Pope Gregory XVI the proper authority to continue the association. Her health was in ruins. She had a growth on her lungs and a serious heart disorder. She had scarcely enough strength to walk.

Pauline and St. Jean Baptiste Vianney, the famous Cure of Ars, were long-time friends. He often visited Lorette to counsel Pauline and seek alms for his projects.

When she asked her physician's permission to go to Rome, he honestly thought she was joking. He gave in but assured her family, "She will not get far."

With two companions, Pauline began the arduous journey. As the party struggled through the snow-covered Alpine passes in an ox cart, it appeared that she would die. However, the iron-willed daughter of Antoine and Jeanne refused to return home and eventually reached Rome. There she accepted the hospitality of the saintly foundress of the Madames of the Sacred Heart, Mere Madeleine Sophie Barat.

In Rome, Mademoiselle Jaricot, exhausted, could not leave her bed. Because she could not visit the pope, her painful trip appeared to have been made in vain. During the long hours of her illness, Pauline and Mere Barat exchanged ideas regarding the social injustice plaguing their homeland. Both women agreed that, unless conditions improved, France would suffer more civil war, death, and destruction. These dark worries gave way before the joyful news that Pope Gregory XVI, aware of Pauline's illness, intended to visit her at the Sacred Heart Convent.

Lorette as it appears today. From here, Pauline and her community, the Daughters of Mary, directed their many projects.

Pope Gregory XVI fostered Pauline's association of the Living Rosary, endowed the prayer group with privileges and indulgences, and used his powerful office to protect Pauline from her clerical and lay detractors.

During the historic audience, Pope Gregory, Mere Barat, and Pauline engaged in lengthy discussions. The pope expressed amazement at Pauline's ingenuity, her grasp of problems of the church, and the practicality with which she addressed them. She advised the pope that the Propagation of the Faith, which was raising great amounts of money, should be established and headquartered in Rome, the center of the Catholic universe. "The papal representative in each country could serve as intermediary for beginning the work in various other countries," she suggested. "Because of the worldwide nature of the Propagation's collections," she added, "it is best to have the movement entirely governed from Rome where the Pilot of the Universal Ship is located."

As the pope left, he remarked to Mere Barat, "How ill she is! She seems to me as if she has come forth from the grave. We will never see her again; she will never return."

Pauline overheard the remark and interjected: "But, Holy Father, if it be God's will, you will see me again. I plan to go to the shrine of Philomena and pray for the restoration of my health. If I were to return to you on foot, Holy Father, would you proceed without delay to the final inquiry into the cause of Philomena's sainthood?"

Five weeks later Pauline, still very ill, left Rome by carriage for the shrine of Philomena in Mugnano, near Naples. Arriving there she was carried into the church by friends. Two days later, during Benediction, she suddenly felt a new surge of life. She stood up and, unassisted, walked out of the church. A few days afterward her heart pains disappeared. At thirty-five years of age she felt the vigor of her youth.

A few days later she knelt before the pope in the Vatican. "Have you come back from the grave?" he asked. The pontiff kept his promise and initiated a study of the cause of Philomena. He gave Pauline permission to build a chapel in her honor in Lyons. (The Sacred Congregation of Rites issued a decree in April, 1961, that abolished local observances on August 10 of the feast of a St. Philomena. The congregation did not officially declare that she was not a saint but that historical evidence of the sanctity was lacking; therefore, the church could not propose her for veneration by the faithful as a saint.)

In May, 1836, Pauline left Rome. "This has been the happiest year of my life," she told friends.

Members of the Lorette community could hardly believe their eyes when Pauline, her health completely restored, returned to Lyons. The Cure of Ars walked to Lyons to see for himself the wonders the intercession of his own patroness, Philomena, had wrought on Pauline's behalf.

*   *   *   *   *

Pope Gregory's gracious welcome and official approval of her zealous and effective work encouraged Pauline and established her credibility in the French church as an apostolic leader. Critics, of course, continued to carp. With increasing frequency, however, church leaders, bishops, priests, religious, and lay persons sought her counsel. Lorette gradually developed into an intellectual and spiritual center for the French church. Missionaries, coming from and going to foreign lands, visited Pauline and never left empty-handed. The social question continued to dominate her thinking, conversation, study, and prayers. In 1839, she returned to Rome to test her slowly maturing plans for a French social reformation. Once more both Pope Gregory XVI and Cardinal Lambruschini promised their support.

Missionary Bishop Charles de Forbin-Janson, while visiting at Lorette, remarked: "I have thousands of babies abandoned in my diocese each year. Pauline, what can we do?"

Once more exercising her genius for breaking the whole into manageable parts, Pauline responded: "Bishop, why don't we ask all the Christian children of France to contribute a half sou a week to save the babies?" This was the beginning of the Association of the Holy Childhood which the bishop formally established in 1843.

In 1839 the Cure of Ars sent Pauline a young lady who had expressed a desire to lead a life of service to the church. "I am going to send you to a Mother who will have great need of you," the Cure told the young woman. "It is Mademoiselle Jaricot, and you must serve her in all her needs." Young Marie Dubouis faithfully fulfilled the Cure's charge. Through all the subsequent joys and sorrows of Pauline Jaricot's life and to the very end of her days, she enjoyed the loyal and loving support of Marie Dubouis.

Pauline, having clarified her vision and established a definite plan of action, judged herself ready to address France's painful social dilemma. She outlined her strategy to the Cure of Ars. "Good Father," she said, "I plan to build a model factory town. The purpose of the town will be to establish a Christian colony to prevent labor abuses, to reward hard work with a just wage, to promote honesty and good Christian spirit among the workers. If the colony prospers, workers can leave there and form other colonies; and so, little by little, town by town, we can spread the gospel principles of social justice."

Pauline's proposal provided workers time for leisure, education, and prayer. Children would have the opportunity for education to their fullest capacity. Her educational system would make it possible for workers' children to enter the professions and thus move out of the laboring class. "Such professionals," she said, "can then turn their talents to assisting the laboring people."

"It is a daring idea, Pauline," the Cure of Ars responded. "It is basically sound and in line with highest Christian idealism." He gave her his blessing and promised continual prayers for the success of the project.

Benefiting from her family's sound business reputation, Pauline quickly raised capital for her new venture from wealthy investors and less affluent factory workers. The moneys thus gathered were deposited in an account poetically entitled "The Bank of Heaven."

Pauline next hired a team of financial advisers: Monsieur Jean-Pierre Allioud and, at his suggestion, Monsieur Gustave Perre. Pauline trusted Allioud implicitly. He had advised her well on various enterprises over the previous years. Gustave Perre, in jail for non-payment of debts when Pauline hired him, was, according to Allioud, "a business genius whose competitors successfully colluded to destroy him." Accepting this judgment, Pauline paid Perre's five-thousand-franc fine and authorities released him from detention. Perre's financial difficulties included the loss during bankruptcy procedures of a factory he had owned in Apt. The property was to be put up for sale. "Why don't we purchase it?" Allioud inquired, ever so gently.

Pauline sent engineers to survey the factory, known as Rustrel. They reported that the soil at the site was rich in iron ore and noted that the plant had "four blast furnaces capable of producing six hundred pounds each per day of top quality iron." Rustrel also boasted a stream, flour mill, and beautiful chapel. Allioud's suggestion to purchase Rustrel seemed to be eminently sound.

Pauline's community at Lorette did not share that judgment. Female intuition told them something was wrong. The women couldn't pin anything down, but they were upset enough to approach Pauline and express their uncertainties, particularly about Perre. "He's a fox," one of them told Pauline. She judged her companions overcautious and defended Perre but, responding to community concern, sought a letter of recommendation for Perre from the parish priest at Apt. The priest wrote a ringing endorsement, thoroughly supporting Allioud's opinion that Gustave Perre was an innocent victim of vicious competitors. "I know his personal affairs thoroughly," the pastor stated. With this letter, Pauline's last misgivings disappeared. "Rustrel is the perfect place to initiate your 'Mission for the Working Man,'" her business team advised. In October, 1845, Pauline invested 500,000 francs to purchase the Rustrel plant and commissioned Perre to be its manager.

The remains of the Rustrel complex:
One of the blast furnaces stands amid
trees and underbrush.

By May, 1846, Pauline discovered that Allioud and Perre had thoroughly conned her. Perre had used Bank of Heaven funds to pay off personal debts and maintain a luxurious lifestyle; his model work force mocked Pauline's vision. She was held accountable for the purchase price of the Rustrel property, 500,000 francs, the interest on that amount since the day of purchase, and the debts contracted by her manager, Perre. She spent the rest of her life trying to fulfill her vow to pay back every penny she owed.

Members of the Jaricot family were prepared to cancel her debts if she would file for bankruptcy, but she steadfastly refused to do so. "I must return the money I borrowed; the money of the rich and the money of the poor," she told them.

Her rich benefactors dunned her fiercely for their money. She sought help from various wealthy families, but in vain. Many felt she should file for bankruptcy and refused to help; others could not help because they themselves were suffering severe financial losses. The poor, who suffered most from their losses, were her greatest comfort and at the same time her greatest source of agony. "They cried for me," she wrote later. One day a little old lady approached her at a railroad station and handed her a rolled-up handkerchief containing two hundred francs. "It is all I have, Pauline, but it is yours," the woman said.

Several French bishops permitted her to collect alms in their dioceses. "Pauline," the bishop of Larochele told her, "the church is eternally in your debt for the three great societies you have founded. I suggest you ask the Propagation of the Faith to help you now. The project at Rustrel was well thought out and has great possibilities for the whole French church. You must not give up. You must continue." The laymen of the ruling council of the Propagation of the Faith, however, rejected her appeal, which she based on her role as foundress of the highly successful fundraising movement. "You never laid claim to the title of foundress of this movement until you found yourself in financial difficulty," the council responded. "Our money is for the missions, not for you." Even an appeal from the pope failed to move the council to change its decision.

The silent and empty Chapel of Our Lady, which Pauline hoped would be the center of the workers' community, bears mute witness to the failure of Pauline's social experiment.

Pauline, in her fifties, her health in ruins, journeyed with Marie Dubouis at her side, from city to city, diocese to diocese, town to town, begging for alms. To save a sou they walked whenever possible. She received support from many sources. John Henry Newman of England recognized her contribution to the church and appealed to the English church on her behalf. Frederick Wilhelm of Prussia gave her a generous donation. Missionary bishops aided her from their meager resources. But it was the poor, with their few sous, who treated her most gently and generously.

Many French clergymen and lay persons openly rejoiced at Pauline's defeat. Long ago they had judged her a meddlesome intruder in a male domain. With the Rustrel fiasco, her critics concluded, she had received precisely what she deserved. There were some who felt she had undertaken the Rustrel venture to increase her personal fortune. These people were especially delighted at the unhappy turn of events. Through all this suffering the Cure of Ars remained her steadfast friend, assisting her with his counsel and prayers.

Several members of the community at Lorette deserted her in the face of these misfortunes. Four remained and, along with her, led a life of complete poverty. Whatever little money they collected went to pay the debts. They sewed vestments and made altar decorations. They cheerfully went without heat, light, and often food. Pauline, despite her own poverty, refused to turn away any poor persons who came to Lorette's door.

In 1852 Pauline sold the Rustrel property at a severe financial loss. After the sale, she still owed 430,000 francs. In February, 1853, the impoverished Pauline applied for public welfare. City authorities issued a certificate stating, "Pauline Marie Jaricot, living on the hill of St.-Barthelemy, is in need and is receiving relief."

In need, indeed. The women at Lorette were so poor they could afford to keep only two tiny oil lamps burning during the evening hours, one in the kitchen and the other in the chapel.

A missionary stopped at Lorette to visit Pauline on one occasion. As the priest left, he offered her six francs for her "good works." She took them, looked hesitantly at him for a moment, and said: "I have no more good works. But may I keep these francs for bread for my household?"

During a public audience with French pilgrims, Pope Pius IX registered public chagrin that Mademoiselle Jaricot had sought financial aid from the

Pauline sold the Rustrel property at a severe loss. Here is the advertisement announcing the sale. Her business failure and consequent indebtedness forced her to seek a pauper's certificate.

Propagation of the Faith. Stung by the pope's remarks, which soon reached her, Pauline, traveling on a pauper's certificate, set out for Rome to obtain an audience with him. At the end of the visit, he said, "Mademoiselle Jaricot, my daughter, it would be an act of justice if the Propagation paid your debts in consideration for all the good you have done for the church. Therefore, I have had my cardinal vicar write to the archbishop of Lyons, asking him to give orders that this should be done."

Despite papal intervention, the council once more refused assistance. The hard-nosed council responded to the pope's plea: "The Propagation does not owe its existence to Mademoiselle Jaricot. Even if it did, it would not be entitled to divert any of its funds to this purpose, since her debts were incurred, not in a work of charity, but in an industrial and commercial enterprise."

As if this public rejection wasn't enough, Pauline suffered insults and harassment from many of her former wealthy benefactors. One wrote her a nasty letter of complaint. Pauline answered, "Your letter cuts me to the heart and I hope you will never know, through your own experience, the timidity which the reproaches of the creditor put in the heart of the one who owes the money. The mystery that enfolds my affair is that of the Cross, my dear Mademoiselle. Your heart does not know what I suffer in not being able to repay you. God knows that when I began I had in mind a great work. My troubles have not changed that intention, but justice must come first."

As she walked through the streets of Lyons, people sometimes called her hypocrite, miser, thief, and other vile names. One day she and Maria visited a poor sick woman. The patient suddenly sat up and pointed a shaking finger at Pauline. "You are justly punished now," the woman shouted, "for the exploits of yours that have failed." The denouncer then commenced a litany of insults and curses. Pauline turned pale, and Maria urged her to leave. Once outside the home, Pauline sobbed, "It's too much, Maria; it's more than I can bear."

Maria suggested a visit to Pauline's old friend, the Cure of Ars. "You have to have confidence in God, Pauline," the Cure counseled, "whatever may happen." The saintly priest gave her a small wooden cross on which was written, "God is my witness, Jesus Christ is my model, Mary is my support. I ask nothing but love and sacrifice."

At the age of sixty-one, Pauline begged God to deliver her from her misery, yet she feared death. "Father," she prayed, "if I cannot pay my debts

The Cure of Ars stood by Pauline through the years of failure. He gave her this cross and offered her the hospitality of his parish.

before I die, grant me the same grace that the good thief had." Although her health worsened, she continued her painful begging tours. Her handwriting grew almost illegible. In a newsletter to Living Rosary members she wrote: "It is pleasant to tell you, my Sisters, that my greatest consolation is to have always submitted to the Holy Catholic Church. My love for the Chair of Peter is, in my eyes, the richest and most precious treasure which God has given me."

Illnesses crowded her. Her heart and lung conditions deteriorated. She suffered dropsy. As body fluid built up within her, she grew heavier and heavier. Doctors advised her that she did not have long to live. Her companions at Lorette lovingly nursed her. The poor, many of whom she had visited, sent her milk, fruits, and sweets. Priests, religious, missionaries, and lay persons prayed for her.

In the latter part of the winter of 1861, Pauline was confined to her cheap, hard bed at Lorette. Only a tiny oil lamp illumined her bare room; no fire cheered it. Yet in her prayers she thanked God for her poverty. But there were times when she journeyed mentally to the rim of despair. She had offered her life as a victim for crimes against the church and for the preservation of the faith in all its purity in her beloved nation. Discouragement and fear fought like demons to possess her heart and convince her of how ridiculous her offering had been. When she received communion, however, peace returned and her lined old face shone with joy.

Ever the businesswoman, she insisted that members of the Lorette community list their personal possessions

This detail from a mural in the Church of St.-Nizier depicts Pauline's four faithful companions who closed her eyes in death. Like her, they persevered to the end.

lest creditors claim the house and all its chattels after her death. She approved each list and in a weak hand signed the women's statements.

As the new year, 1862, dawned, it was evident that Pauline Jaricot had entered the last days of her life. She prayed constantly for France, for sinners, for pardon of her own trespasses. Early in the morning of January 9, she cried out, "Mary, my Mother, I am all yours!" These were her last words. "Her face," a bystander noted, "became calm and young as death approached. Her lips bore a faint smile." Two days later she was buried in Lyons. Many people — religious, priests, lay people, the rich, the poor — attended her funeral. The women of her household accompanied the pauper's coffin to the family crypt. Cardinal Villecourt said of her: "Perhaps in heaven she will obtain the conversion of those who were her oppressors and who made her undergo a long period of dying." After her death, the family sold the property at Lorette and satisfied all her creditors.

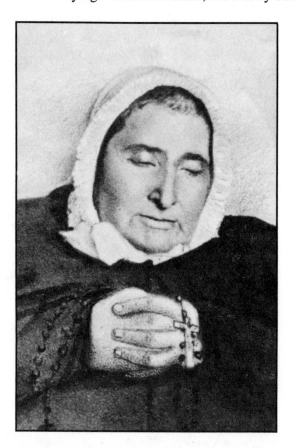

In June, 1930, Pope Pius XI signed the official decree opening the cause of the beatification of Pauline Jaricot, which is still in process.

Edema caused Pauline's face to swell during her last years. She died peacefully on January 9, 1862.

Teresa of Avila

She was the daughter of his smiles and his tears. Half-angel, half-imp, Teresa de Cepeda y Ahumada, during her first sixteen years on this earth, had caused her father more joy and more worry than all his ten other children. On this hot July evening in 1531, Don Alonso, Teresa's father, sat disconsolate in the study of his fine home in Avila, Spain. The loneliness he now felt surprised him. It had been a hard day for Don Alonso and an even harder one for his favorite daughter, Teresa. That morning he had placed Teresa in a convent boarding school just outside the great sand-colored battlements ringing Avila. Don Alonso had put off the decision for months. A widower of two years, he was deeply attached to his sixteen-year-old Teresa. He was a somber and melancholy man, and his daughter's joyful and affectionate ways had filled the deep void left in his life by the death of his wife, Beatriz.

As he tried to shake off his sadness, Don Alonso's glance moved over his well-appointed study and came to rest on the chess table. The chess set — knights, bishops, pawns and rooks, queens and kings — stood in battle array, awaiting human hands and minds, to order them into battle. Don Alonso had taught the game to Teresa, and the two often engaged each other in spirited matches. It would be many months before her triumphant cry "Check!" would

179

once again echo through the room.

Don Alonso was not the only one who missed Teresa. Among the youth of Avila's more prosperous families, Teresa's quick mind, sense of humor, and sparkling laughter enlivened many a social event. Teresa was always up to something. She was a born instigator, a trait she manifested as early as the age of seven, when she had enticed her brother Rodrigo into one of her madcap adventures.

The escapade started when Don Alonso had obtained some beautifully illustrated volumes of the lives of the saints for his children. Teresa, born on March 28, 1515, and her favorite brother, Rodrigo, eleven, four years older than Teresa, spent hours reading the precious volumes. The procession of valiant monks, pious popes, and gracious virgins that marched serenely across the illustrated pages captivated the two. The martyrs, most of all, intrigued Teresa. "They were smart," the young scholar concluded. "They got to heaven right away." And heaven, she was sure at that age, was *the* place to be. In later life, recounting this incident, she wrote: "I openly desired to die as a martyr. I did not want this on account of the love I felt for God, but to enjoy very quickly the wonderful things I had read there were in heaven."

During Teresa's time any Christian who desired martyrdom on demand could go to Morocco. The country belonged to the Moors, followers of the Mohammedan religion. Christians and Moors had been killing each other in the name of their respective religions for centuries. The faithful of both sides were convinced that death at the hands of the other earned them immediate eternal joy.

Teresa lived her life within and around the massive medieval battlements of Avila, in north central Spain.

"Rodrigo, you and I have first got to get to Morocco if we want to get to heaven," Teresa advised her brother. It didn't bother the little one that she and Rodrigo would have to journey for two weeks halfway through Spain and then across the Mediterranean to reach Morocco. "Once we get there, the Moors will cut off our heads and we will be in heaven forever and ever. Just think, Rodrigo, forever and ever." Whatever Rodrigo did think, it did not stop him from joining Teresa in her holy venture. Before the next morning light, the two adventurers slipped out of the de Cepeda home, passed through the city's gates, and began their journey into destiny. When only a short distance outside Avila's walls, they halted to pray at a wayside shrine.

As the two children were praying, the sun came up and Beatriz and Don Alonso discovered the little ones' absence. Terror seized the parents. Don Alonso felt sure the children had fallen into a well and drowned or had been kidnapped. "Children lost!" the dread cry rose from person to person, from home to home.

The "Four Posts," a wayside shrine, overlooks Avila's turrets and towers. Here Teresa and her brother Rodrigo made what turned out to be the last stop on their brave youthful journey to martyrdom.

As it echoed through Avila's cobblestone streets it sent a chill into the hearts of the city's awakening citizens.

As the alarm was sounding in Avila, a horseman, unaware of the uproar in town, approached the shrine and noticed Teresa and Rodrigo praying. He soon recognized the little ones, and they recognized him. He was their uncle, Francisco. Within a few moments Francisco placed the two children on his horse and shortly after returned them home. Teresa and Rodrigo had lost their bid for martyrdom; no Moors would cut off their heads. But no doubt they both had a sound spanking before the day was out.

The setback did nothing to dampen Teresa's enthusiasm for holy enterprise. Next she was talking Rodrigo into being a hermit. "Hermits can't be hermits, Rodrigo," she wisely observed, "unless they have hermitages. Go to the orchard behind the house and build a hermitage for each of us." Poor Rodrigo proved no better an architect than martyr. The hermitages he so laboriously built collapsed one by one. With their fall all Teresa's hopes of finding holiness as a solitary disappeared.

Perhaps her path lay in community life. So now the young Teresa, envisioning herself as superior of a religious community, organized her playmates into male and female religious orders. Their purpose was to raise money for the poor. Borrowing some of her mother's old dresses, "Mother Foundress" sewed habits for her "religious" and dispatched them to beg alms through Avila for the poor. Teresa's mendicants did indeed raise money, which she cheerfully distributed among Avila's poor.

Teresa found her inspiration for all these endeavors in the lives of the saints she continued to read. Sometime during her eighth or ninth year, however, her interests shifted from these biographies to the then popular romantic novels. These tales of heroic knights, damsels in distress, evil princes, and villainous knaves were the soap operas of Teresa's time. Her mother Beatriz probably introduced young Teresa to these sentimental stories. Before long both mother and daughter were hooked on them. Don Alonso, dismayed by this change in Teresa's reading habits, chided his wife and daughter. "Your mind should be occupied with more serious thoughts," the father complained. The two, infatuated with the silly novels, continued to devour them. They were wise enough to hide the precious volumes from Don Alonso.

These cheerful days of Teresa's young life came to an abrupt and painful end when Beatriz died. Teresa's mother was only in her early thirties. Teresa, fourteen, was desolate. She wept continuously. Loneliness soaked her heart.

*　　*　　*　　*　　*

Beatriz died when Teresa needed her most. The young girl stood on the threshold of life. "I was very vain," she later recalled. She had reason to be. Of medium height, Teresa possessed a beautifully shaped face, clear white skin, crowned with black shining hair. When she smiled, which was often, her black eyes danced and sparkled. The charming, graceful Teresa knew how to dress and spared no pains to wear her fine clothing and exquisite jewelry to best advantage. Well coordinated in mind and body, she was both a fine horsewoman and witty conversationalist. When her father introduced her to Avila's social life, more than one young man's head spun; more than one young woman's heart hung heavy with envy.

Don Alonso, although proud of his daughter, had some reason for concern. He was troubled about some of Teresa's companions. He felt particularly uneasy

Teresa's father, Don Alonso, returned home by the path to the right after he enrolled his daughter in school at the convent of Our Lady of Grace.

about her relationship with one girl cousin. Writing of this stage of her life, Teresa noted, "I dared to do many things, truly against my honor and God." The statement is enigmatic, and Teresa never clarifies precisely what she meant by "many things." Whatever they were, they could not have been serious enough to ruin her reputation. Gossip traveled fast in the tight circles of Avila's society. And Don Alonso was worried. Shortly after the forthcoming marriage of his eldest daughter, Maria, was announced, Don Alonso managed to enroll Teresa in the convent boarding school of Our Lady of Grace just outside Avila's walls. There would be no older woman at home to guide the sixteen-year-old Teresa, and Don Alonso did not feel equal to the task.

At first Teresa hated the convent school. Her former companions kept sending notes until the nuns discreetly shut off communications. The sisters conducted the convent school with strict discipline. The girls spent their time at prayer, learning embroidery and needlework, studying religion, and recreating according to a strict regimen. Although the independent, haughty, spoiled Teresa did not adjust readily, she soon perceived that the sisters with whom she lived were loving people. Her headmistress, Sister Maria Briceno, particularly impressed the motherless girl; so deeply indeed that the young lady thought seriously about entering religious life herself. The more she considered this possibility, however, the more she hated it. "I asked God not to give me this vocation," she later wrote. Despite her prayer for another vocation, the attraction for religious life refused to disappear and Teresa spent agonizing months of indecision.

The battle drained Teresa's energy, and a year and a half after entering the convent school she suffered a severe illness and returned home to her father. During her ensuing convalescence, her uncle Pedro, an old man who spent much time in prayer and spiritual reading, asked Teresa to read certain religious books to him. Although the prospect annoyed her, she loved her uncle and was happy to do whatever she could to please him. So she complied with his request. The books, dealing with the vanity of the world, the nothingness of all earthly things, the meaning of life, death, and afterlife, forced Teresa to confront herself. Tired of the inner warfare that sapped her energy, undermined her health, and destroyed her normal zest for life, Teresa made her decision. She would be a nun. "I decided," she wrote, "to force myself to accept it."

A new and unexpected obstacle now loomed in Teresa's path. Much to her surprise, Don Alonso, a deeply religious man, forbade her to enter the convent.

"After I am dead," he advised, "you can do what you please . . ." The father should have known that once his headstrong little girl made up her mind, nothing could stop her. On the second of November, 1535, the twenty-year-old Teresa repeated her early morning escape of childhood. She left home before dawn and walked through Avila's battlements, down the steep hill to the convent of the Incarnation. This large monastery, only a brief walk from Avila, belonged to the Carmelite Sisters of the Mitigated Observance. We do not know why Teresa chose the Carmelites in preference to the Augustinians of her convent school days. She did have a dear friend who had entered the Incarnation a short time before. Further, this Carmelite life, while austere, was not as severe as that of the Augustinians. And Teresa may have felt that she could fit in better at the Incarnation.

If we do not know her motives for choosing the Carmelites, we do know that the separation from her father, Don Alonso, cost her dearly. "When I left my father's house," she writes, "it seemed every bone in my body was being sundered." After a brief bout of anger, Don Alonso accepted the inevitable, reconciled himself to his daughter, and provided her with a generous dowry for her new life in the convent.

*   *   *   *   *

Young Sister Teresa of Jesus, as she was called, was indeed a bundle of contradictions. She had entered the convent, not so much out of love of God, but because she believed the religious life was the best means for her to save her soul. She was still the little child who was willing to have her head

Teresa spent the first twenty-seven years of her religious life at the Carmelite Incarnation Convent.

cut off, not so much for love of God as for the reward of heaven. Stubborn, proud, independent, and not yet willing to surrender her heart to God, Teresa was nevertheless dutiful, selfless, chaste, and conscientious. She spent many long hours chanting the Divine Office with her sisters, but continually botched her halfhearted attempts at private prayer. Outwardly Teresa was a smiling, cheerful sister, witty and warm. Deep inside herself, however, she was distressed and ill at ease with her failure to deepen her relationship with God and mature in her spiritual life.

Despite the inner conflict, she experienced a certain peace that kept her going — almost. Two years after entering the Incarnation, Teresa experienced a series of fainting spells accompanied by severe cardiac pain and high fever. After several remedies failed, physicians in Avila advised the Carmelite superiors and the worried Don Alonso they could do nothing to cure Teresa. The desperate father arranged with Teresa's superiors to bring his daughter to a woman healer who lived in the town of Becedas, several miles west of Avila.

For three months the healer purged, bled, pummeled, and injected the sick young nun. Teresa's body, beaten and bruised, was a well of pain. So sensitive was her skin that the slightest touch would cause her severe pain. After three months of this treatment the young patient lapsed into what appeared to be a deep coma. The nuns keeping vigil at her bedside were convinced young Teresa had died; and, according to the custom of the region, they dripped wax from the candles used in her final anointing over

The oratory at the Incarnation Convent was the arena of Teresa's two-decade struggle to achieve inner peace and spiritual growth. "I had to muster up all my courage to go there," she writes.

her closed eyes. Back at the Incarnation, the superiors had a grave opened to receive the body of the young sister. Don Alonso alone, who sat by his daughter during all these terrible hours, refused to accept Teresa's death and to permit the sisters to remove her body. "This girl is not for the grave," he said over and over again. After four days of coma, Teresa regained consciousness. Although the illness and unsuccessful treatment had ravaged her body and spirit, Teresa insisted upon returning to the convent of the Incarnation as soon as possible. Don Alonso brought his daughter back around Easter, 1540. She was fever-parched, full of pain, and paralyzed. Sister Teresa of Jesus would not walk for three long years.

All during her years of harrowing physical suffering, Teresa's spiritual struggle dragged on. Dilemmas remained unresolved. Teresa wanted to love God completely but kept holding back. She prayed often but found little consolation. She tried to put herself in the presence of God; but when she did, she experienced sadness. "I remember the favors the Lord had granted me in prayer and how badly I was repaying him . . . ."

Paralyzed both physically and spiritually, the young nun could find neither a physician for her broken body nor a director for her sorely tried spirit. Only her innate stubbornness sustained her. Refusing to remain immovable from the paralysis, Teresa dragged herself from place to place within the convent on her hands and knees. "Since I saw myself so crippled and still so young, and saw how helpless the doctors of the earth were, I recommended myself to St. Joseph," she remembered. As far as she was concerned, it was St. Joseph who restored her health to the extent she could walk and return to full community life at the Incarnation. It was not the first nor indeed the last time Teresa de Cepeda y Ahumada would call upon Joseph and he would respond.

If the physical cure came quickly, the spiritual one did not. For the next eighteen years, Teresa floundered. Her attempts at prayer became lengthy exercises in frustration. Trying to improve, she set a definite hour each day for private prayer. She endured the long sixty minutes only by turning the pages of the Bible and waiting for the clock to strike, indicating her time had elapsed. Her only satisfaction was that she had put her time in. "I preferred a heavy penance rather than to recollect myself in the practice of prayer," she admitted.

But this determined woman refused to surrender. Her courage ("I have more than most women," she boasted) would not tolerate defeat. After nearly two decades, during which she suffered physical breakdown, depression, lack of proper direction, and an endless series of spiritual defeats, Teresa began to experience some peace of heart. As God's presence within her own heart made itself more clearly felt, Teresa began to grasp the source of her spiritual shabbiness. It was her own stubborn pride that made her ashamed to be in the presence of her Lord because she was sinful. For all her life the independent Teresa had attempted to bring God into her life on her own terms, which demanded that she be as perfect as possible before she could be comfortable in God's presence. When she realized that Christ was asking her to depend on his love, which was so strong that he would accept her just as she was, sins and all, her new life dawned. Years before, she had read in a book by the great Franciscan spiritual writer Father Francisco de Osuna that no deepening of one's relationship with God was possible unless "you enter into yourself." Now Osuna's advice took on new import for Teresa. She prayed for the grace of being at ease in the Lord's presence regardless of her sinfulness. She practiced a little stratagem. "I strove to picture Christ within me," she reveals, "and it did me greater good in my opinion to picture him in those scenes where I saw him more alone. It seems to me that, being alone and afflicted as a person in need, he had to accept me. . . .

In the convent garden, Teresa often joined in recreation with her fellow sisters. On the surface she was a well-adjusted nun; underneath she was confused and bewildered.

The scene of his prayers in the Garden was a special comfort to me. I strove to be his companion there. I decided to wipe away the sweat he so painfully experienced. But I recall that I never dared to actually do it because my sins appeared to be so serious."

Teresa had begun to force open the door to her inner self. She was soon to find there the meaning of Christ's words, "The kingdom of God is within you."

As she opened her heart more and more to the presence of God, a great fear seized Teresa. It threatened to destroy all her new-found peace. The nun worried that all her present awareness of God's presence, all her sense of spiritual progress, could possibly be a bitter delusion. "Was it the work of the devil or of the Holy Spirit?" she worried. Her fears were not groundless. A series of bizarre events connected with women mystics had shaken the Spanish church. The Spanish hierarchy had revealed that certain women, highly regarded because

of their visions, and in some cases, stigmata, were frauds. Some actually practiced devil-worship. These ingenious women had deceived every level of Spanish society, including bishops and royalty. People now looked skeptically upon anyone who claimed to have any special relationship with God or any special prayer experiences.

Teresa, at first convinced that she was moving to an ever closer and more intense union with God, now wasn't so sure. She needed a spiritual director for advice and support. She turned to two priest friends who, after listening to her describe her prayer life, concluded her new-found experience could only be the

A steel engraving from a seventeenth-century book on Teresa of Avila's spiritual teachings portrays scenes from Christ's passion. Teresa started to make sense of her own life when she began meditating on Christ's human sufferings.

devil's work. "You could give up all your faults and failings at once if it was from God," one priest piously declared. The two well-meaning and holy priests then made the mistake of consulting other eminent and holy people regarding Teresa's dilemma. Neither priest ever mentioned anything Teresa said in confession, but they did speak of her spiritual suffering.

When word got about Avila that something strange was occurring with Sister Teresa of Jesus, citizens watched to see if yet another religious quack was about to emerge on the Spanish scene. Teresa's sincere but fumbling spiritual directors now put her through a terrible wringer. They ordered her never to be alone, lest the devil should overwhelm her. She often complained of incompetent spiritual advisers. "I fear them more than I do the devil," she wrote. Relief, fortunately, was not long in coming. A humble Jesuit priest, Father de Centina, a young man of twenty-three, half Teresa's age at this time, undertook to guide the troubled nun.

Father de Cetina had the proper combination of prudence, intelligence, and optimism to direct Teresa. Father Francis Borgia, another Jesuit who was later canonized, heard her confession and counseled her. Both priests assured Teresa that the spirit of God *was* at work within her. "I was very much relieved," Teresa noted. Jesuits continued to direct her within the next two years as her mystical experiences multiplied and intensified. She was aware of Christ standing beside her; she experienced his presence in his resurrected body; Christ spoke with her.

One day she sensed his love so strongly she felt as if her heart was

Teresa highly esteemed Francis Borgia, noted Jesuit priest and spiritual writer. He directed her for two years, giving her wise counsel as her mystical experiences multiplied and intensified.

pierced. It was no wild imagining. When Teresa died, years after this experience, an autopsy revealed her heart bore a hole through its center as if it had been pierced by a dart. Teresa discovered that as she emptied herself of worldly concerns, she had more room in her "interior castle" for the love of God.

Her spiritual directors constantly cross-examined and encouraged her — and scratched their heads over her. Father Baltasar Alvarez, another Jesuit counselor of Teresa, one day showed a confrere a great pile of spiritual books cluttering his room and groaned, "I read all these, trying to understand Teresa of Jesus."

*   *   *   *   *

In August, 1560, when Teresa was forty-five, Peter of Alcantara, an austere Franciscan who had reformed the friars in Spain and who was eventually canonized, visited Teresa and assured her that the spirit of God was indeed favoring her. After encouraging her to continue her prayer life, he expressed his deep sorrow for Teresa. "One of the greatest afflictions on earth, one that I suffered as I struggled to renew the Franciscan order," the saint explained, "is the opposition of good men. Plenty of that, Teresa," Peter sighed, "is still in store for you."

As Teresa progressed in her spiritual growth, she yearned to share her new-found joy with others. Looking back over her spiritual odyssey, she knew she had arrived at a critical juncture when she accepted the spiritual

Peter of Alacantra, an austere Franciscan who had reformed the friars in Spain, assured Teresa that the spirit of God was favoring her but cautioned her that "the opposition of good men" lay in store for her if she undertook the reformation of the Carmelites.

writer Osuna's advice to "enter into yourself." In that same passage the author explained that one seeking a life of intense prayer must also seek quiet and solitude. "The secluded place will awaken you and invite you to make the inward journey," Osuna observed.

Teresa knew there were nuns at the Incarnation who desired a deeper prayer life. But the Carmelite convent was hardly the "secluded place" Osuna recommended. Two hundred people, including nuns, relatives, and servants lived within the Incarnation. The nuns, mostly from Avila, entertained numerous visitors of both sexes. Since the sisters were not strictly cloistered, they were free to visit the city and its environs. Little went on at the Incarnation that wasn't gossiped about in Avila; little occurred in Avila that wasn't gossiped about in the Incarnation.

While all this was acceptable under the Mitigated Carmelite Rule as it was observed in Teresa's time, it was hardly what St. Albert of Jerusalem had in mind when he had established the primitive Carmelite Rule three centuries previously. That saint, leading his followers in lives of prayer, penance, silence, and seclusion, insisted that Carmelite communities of both friars and nuns be small in number. The nuns were strictly cloistered. Visitors were few and could only speak to the sisters through a grille.

To obtain her "secluded place" and to initiate a return to the primitive Carmelite Rule, Teresa decided to take a bold step. She sought permission to establish in Avila, under the patronage of St. Joseph, a small community of nuns that would number no more than thirteen. The sisters would live a life of prayer and seclusion, as the primitive Carmelite Rule enjoined. A wealthy widow in town, Dona Guiomar de Ulloa, agreed to assist Teresa and began to search for a small house in Avila for the new foundation.

At first Father Gregory Fernandez, who as superior of the Carmelite friars was also Teresa's superior, warmed to the idea. "He is fond of all religious life," Teresa cheerfully observed.

When word leaked out at the Incarnation and in Avila of the proposed convent, a storm broke over Teresa's and Fernandez's heads. The nuns at the Incarnation looked upon Teresa's move as an affront to their own religious lifestyle and a threat to the unity of the Carmelite Order. "I was very much disliked throughout my own monastery," Teresa remembered. Since many people in Avila had relatives at the Incarnation, they shared the sisters' indignation. Moreover, citizens of Avila, who were presently supporting a disproportionate number of convents and monasteries, were dismayed at the prospect of having one more religious house depending on their bounty.

Opposition grew vocal and violent. Rumor mounted upon rumor. Teresa, it was reported, was bold and defiant. She was, moreover, having revelations. Inevitably the gossips compared her to the fake mystics who had caused so much trouble only a few years before. "We suffered from gossip and derision," Teresa recalled. "I did not know what to do."

Father Fernandez knew what to do. Overpowered by the mounting criticism, he withdrew the permission he had given to Teresa to open her new convent. It looked like the end of the "secluded place." But Teresa now found an ally from a most unexpected quarter. Don Alvaro de Mendoza, Bishop of Avila, a friend of Peter Alcantara, threw his support behind Teresa. Moved by Peter's plea, the bishop, with the approval of Pope Pius IV, offered to take the new foundation under his jurisdiction. It was a courageous gesture that baffled and further inflamed Teresa's foes. Father Fernandez accused the bishop of going over his head and judged Teresa a rebellious nun. The bishop was risking much by supporting Teresa. Her attempt to restore the primitive Carmelite Rule cast her in the role of a "holier-than-thou" innovator. Her enemies compared Teresa to the Protestant Reformers of northern Europe, whom the Spanish feared.

Luther and his fellow reformers justified their actions on two scores. First, they claimed they were leading the people of God in a return to primitive Christianity. Second, they claimed to be purging the church of a corrupt and indifferent clergy. Teresa was doing, in her enemies' judgment, exactly the same thing within the Carmelite Order. She was proclaiming a return to primitive Carmelite life, and she was purging the Incarnation convent. Her opponents' anger and frustration arose from their belief that there was, first, no need to return to the primitive Carmelite Rule since the present Carmelite sisters were observing their updated Mitigated Rule. Further, the sisters at the Incarnation could hardly be termed corrupt. Just as the Reformers had led nation after nation out of the Catholic church and destroyed the political and religious unity of Europe, so Teresa's foes claimed that she, too, would eventually destroy the present unity of the Carmelite Order.

The Spanish kings of Teresa's time felt Catholicism was the one force that welded their nation together. Any threat to the Catholic religion became, in the eyes not only of the king but of the people, a threat to the Spanish nation. The

Carmelites were a well-respected and beloved segment of the Catholic church in the Spain of Teresa's day. And now this upstart nun was meddling with the whole structure of the order. It was not a threat that any Spaniard would take lightly. To preserve Catholic unity, the crown had some years before established the office of the Inquisition.

This institution, composed of learned theologians, investigated any possible harmful influences in Spain. The crown meant business. Only two years before Teresa made her move, Spanish authorities had burned at the stake Spanish priests and nuns who had refused to renounce their adherence to Lutheranism.

It was against this background of political and religious turmoil, and in an atmosphere charged with fear and suspicion, that Teresa initiated the primitive Carmelite movement at St. Joseph's in Avila, August 24, 1562. On that morning the priest Maester Daza, in the name of the bishop, clothed four novices in rough serge habits Teresa herself had designed and sewn. The reform was under way.

St. Joseph's Convent in Avila, Teresa's first foundation, provided the proper setting for the prayer and penitential life she desired. It eventually became the center of the great Carmelite reform.

No sooner had the first Mass in the little convent been concluded than a mob of Avila's citizens pounded on the door, threatening to invade St. Joseph's and throw out the nuns. For some moments the crowd hurled threats and curses at the sisters and then inexplicably withdrew. City officials called several town meetings. Emotions ran high. But Teresa refused to withdraw the nuns from the convent. Both sides sent lobbies to the Spanish capital, Madrid, in an attempt to seek royal support for their respective positions. By the following spring, 1563, stubborn Sister Teresa of Jesus still had her convent functioning. The Carmelite Provincial finally recognized her as its Superior. He even permitted four nuns from the Incarnation to join her community. Within a short time the little convent numbered the thirteen sisters that Teresa desired. At this time Teresa entered one of the happiest periods of her life.

Now, finally, at forty-eight years of age, Teresa had found meaning for her life. She had discovered her mission and had the means to accomplish it. Her mission — to lead her sisters in a life of prayer for the church of her day. Corroding from its own inner corruption, and staggering under the blows of the Protestant Reformation, the Roman Catholic church was making a sincere effort at self-renewal. The Council of Trent had clearly established the paths that had to be followed. Philip II, King of Spain and Europe's most powerful monarch, had thrown all his prestige and resources into implementing the decrees of Trent throughout his vast empire. Teresa, and Philip, too, knew that without prayer no amount of political, military, or ecclesiastical power could save the church. Thus Teresa and her sisters aimed to witness, through their lives of prayer, the truth that God is the source of all life, strength, and power.

St. Joseph's Convent provided the "secluded place" where Teresa's prayer life could flourish. The tiny community lived in severe poverty, fasted, abstained from meat, slept on rough straw beds, and engaged in manual labor. Distractions such as visitors were kept at a minimum. Whatever contributed to the atmosphere of prayer was encouraged; what did not was rejected.

*   *   *   *   *

In November, 1568, the fifty-three-year-old Teresa experienced the fulfillment of her heart's desire. She requested and obtained permission from the Carmelite General to establish monasteries of Primitive Observance for Carmelite friars. After almost a year she found a humble house in a remote Spanish farm area for the project. A little later she discovered two Carmelite friars willing to undertake the project: one, Father Antonio de Heredia, a well-respected Carmelite; and the second, a boyish-looking Carmelite priest, twenty-five-year-old Father John of the Cross de Yepes, who was one day to be canonized. The two priests, combining a life of prayer and apostolic work among the farm people, were extremely happy with their new life. As yet the Lord did not show them how much they would have to suffer for his name. The prophecy of Peter of Alcantara was about to fall upon Teresa with renewed vengeance.

Father Angel de Salazar, the new Carmelite Provincial, shared the dismay of his predecessor, Father Fernandez, at Teresa's success. He yearned to hobble the swiftly moving nun. Her recent efforts to initiate the Carmelite renewal among the friars particularly irritated him. Salazar hit upon a clever ploy. In the Chapter of 1571 he appointed Teresa Prioress of the Incarnation Convent in Avila. By this one deed he hoped to check her reforming zeal for at least the three years her term as prioress of the Incarnation would require. He also guessed she would exhaust herself in what he presumed would be an exercise in futility — the introduction of the Primitive Reform at the Incarnation.

Teresa suffered deep anguish when Salazar informed her of her appointment. She would have to abandon the new convents she had started. She knew, too, she would be the center of controversy at the Incarnation. The day she came to accept her office only proved how right she was. Teresa's opponents among the

On her journeys throughout Spain to establish new convents of the reform, Teresa often met with Fathers Antonio de Heredia and John of the Cross, the pioneers of the male Carmelite reform.

nuns there, joined by their relatives from Avila, greeted their new superior with hoots, catcalls, and threats of physical harm. There was, however, within the Incarnation a group of nuns who determined to support Teresa. These sisters realized the convent was in serious trouble. The spirit of prayer had disappeared, discipline had relaxed, visitors abounded, funds had been depleted to such an extent that the nuns did not have enough to eat. Many took their daily meals with relatives in Avila.

Teresa determined to do the best job she could. And with her typical common sense she began her reform by providing enough food for the table. One by one, carefully and prudently, she faced an endless series of problems. She brought in Father John of the Cross as confessor for the sisters. As a friar of the Primitive Observance, his presence in such a sensitive role caused great upset within the community. Eventually the sisters accepted him. Under his direction, Teresa herself and many of the sisters began to grow in the spirit of God.

Convinced that the Incarnation's financial troubles stemmed from its loss of the spirit of prayer, Teresa gradually shut off the flow of visitors from Avila

When John of the Cross joined Teresa's reform, she taught him its rule and spirit. Under his direction, she and the other sisters began to grow in the spirit of God.

and its environs. During Lent of 1572, for example, the Incarnation nuns had absolutely no visitors!

Father Salazar's hope of keeping Teresa out of action for three years came to naught when the Spanish king, Philip II, using his power and prestige, interceded to have Teresa attend to various matters concerning the Reformed Carmelites. Within a year and a half of her assuming the leadership of the Incarnation, Teresa's duties were effectively ended there. Now she could get back to the unfinished work of establishing the Reform.

*   *   *   *   *

During these busy years of pioneering, Teresa was engaged in a second and no less demanding career. She was writing. Her literary life began in her mid-forties and hit high gear in her fifties and sixties. Before she died she had written eleven books and twenty-three poems. This number does not count her book on chivalry which she co-authored with her brother Rodrigo when they were children. One biographer who read the book maintains it was surprisingly well written.

Scholars estimate Teresa wrote over fifteen thousand letters. Over five hundred of these are preserved, and they give a glimpse into the heart of this magnificent woman. She frankly admits to her spiritual director Father Gracian, who was away on a journey, how lonely she is for him. She sends him numerous poems to cheer him up. To a Jesuit who accused her of being proud,

During the tumultuous years of foundation, Father Jerome Gracian served as Teresa's spiritual mentor and religious superior.

she writes, "I am not humble enough to relish being called proud — nor do I think you should parade your own humility at my expense." Her good humor keeps bubbling up in these letters. It is rare that her personal illness, trials, and troubles depress her for any length of time. But it does happen and she is not afraid to admit, "I am depressed." She begins one letter, "I can't seem to shake it."

Prophetically Teresa told a Carmelite priest: "Many souls will profit after I am dead from what I am writing." Over a period of four centuries more than 2,160 editions of her books have appeared in at least twenty-two different languages. These writings, including her celebrated book of mystical theology, *Interior Castle*, are an incredible achievement — all the more so when one recalls that her literary career began and reached its zenith during the last twenty-five years of her life.

*   *   *   *   *

Despite the knowledge that the emperor, Philip II, and the bishop of Avila supported Teresa's work, her enemies continued to harass her and her followers at every turn. Foes spread malicious gossip about her and her relations with priests and friars. They scorned her endless travels. "She walls up everybody else in the cloister," they complained, "and travels all over Spain herself." The papal nuncio, His Excellency Philip Sega, described her as "a restless, gadabout woman, preaching as a mistress, against the orders of St. Paul, who has forbidden women to teach in the Church."

Her supporters at times disappointed her. More than once her plans concerning the reformation of convents and monasteries went awry when priests, friars, and nuns upon whom she depended failed her. But despite all this, the reform continued and progressed. By 1576 friars of the Primitive Rule, called the Discalced since they went barefoot, numbered over seventy-five. Under the leadership of Father Gracian, they attempted to establish their own province.

Carmelite authorities reacted violently, judging Gracian's move rebellious. The heavy fist of authority came down hardest on the gentle John of the Cross at the Incarnation convent. Mitigated Friars kidnapped him and slammed him into a six-by-ten-foot cell in a Carmelite monastery in Toledo. They scourged him to blood several times a week, and cut off any communication he had with the outside world. He was forbidden books or writing materials and could not celebrate Mass. He was given nothing but bread, water, and sardines for nourishment; his captors refused him a clean tunic. His rough serge habit was matted with his own blood. The garment clung to the wounds from the frequent scourging. He would bear the marks of these beatings on his body until his death. Yet it was during these days of isolation, suffering, and rejection that John of the Cross wrote one of the most beautiful religious love poems in Spanish literature, called *The Dark Night of the Soul*. He composed the verses in his cell and memorized them. Finally, after nineteen months of this punishment, John escaped and was able to write down the verses.

But John returned to a new and fresh disaster. The blundering leader of the Carmelite Reform, Father Gracian, had proclaimed once more — despite the pleas of Teresa and John of the Cross that this was not the time — that the reformed Carmelites would establish a separate province in Spain. This was an act of rebellion and Rome repudiated it. The papal nuncio had Gracian excommunicated and imprisoned. All Teresa's work seemed doomed.

She had not counted on Philip II. He had invited her, in the year 1577, to come to his new palace, called the Escorial, outside Madrid. During this interview he was able to assess the value of this woman who sat before him. She won him completely to her side. After this excommunication was hurled against Father Gracian, Philip called in the papal nuncio and, in a rare display of anger, demanded that the nuncio conduct an impartial investigation of the Primitive Carmelite Reform movement and Teresa's work. The nuncio did just that and soon realized he had been prejudiced from the beginning by the Carmelite parent organization's opinion of Teresa and the reform movement. He recommended to the pope that the reform be permitted to establish a separate province of its own in Spain. The pope concurred. Teresa, the indomitable and stubborn Spanish lady, had finally triumphed.

*   *   *   *   *

Teresa's life work of establishing the Primitive Carmelite Reform was now on a firm and solid basis. The task completed, the Lord now prepared her for death. One by one the strings that bound her to earth were cut. First, it was her beauty. In the fall of 1581, Teresa fell victim to a frightful influenza epidemic that swept over Spain. She survived, but her health was broken and, for the first time, she lost her youthful face. "You would be shocked," she wrote a friend, "to see how old I am . . . ." She grew more and more feeble as an internal cancer inexorably destroyed her physical strength.

Next, the bonds of family were affected. She was proud of her ancestry. All during her life she had remained close to many members of her family. Unfortunately the tight family structure had suffered a severe blow when her brother Lorenzo died in June of 1580. Lorenzo, a wealthy man, loved Teresa and named her executrix of his will. In that testament he left her a large sum of money to construct a chapel for the tiny convent of St. Joseph's in Avila. Many members of the family were jealous of this bequest and others that Lorenzo had made. Most of their anger was directed at Teresa. She was torn between trying to placate the family and conscientiously observe what Lorenzo had willed. "All this business of the will is killing me," she complained in a letter to a friend.

But perhaps the unkindest cut of all came when Teresa, just two months before she died, began her final journey from Burgos to Avila. She had hoped to reach the town of her birth before she died. But so ill was she that she stopped at a convent in Valladolid. Her stay there was highly unpleasant. The community loved her dearly, but its Superior, Sister Maria Bautista, a niece of Teresa's, had sided against her in the matter of Lorenzo's will. Years before, Maria and Teresa had been very close. And when the young girl entered the Carmelite convent of the Reform, Teresa had bestowed great love and interest upon her. But because of Lorenzo's will, poor Teresa now experienced such coldness and disdain from Maria that she could hardly wait to leave the Valladolid convent.

In mid-September, Teresa was able to resume her journey to Avila. Before leaving the Valladolid convent, she called the community together and bade them farewell in terms most tender. After Teresa's little speech, Maria Bautista accompanied her from the chapel to the front door of the convent. And then she addressed the final harsh words to Teresa: "Get out of this house," Maria Bautista said, "and never return."

At the last, Teresa was denied the sight of her beloved Avila. After she left Valladolid, on her way home she was summoned to Alba de Tormes to tend to someone who felt she needed Teresa very badly. Teresa responded to the summons and got as far as the convent in town, where she had to rest. She lingered there for weeks, and on the eve of the feast of St. Francis, 1582, the sisters knew that the end was near. They heard the indomitable lady singing sweetly. Her face looked young and beautiful. She advised the sisters that death was imminent.

The priest who anointed her asked her where she wished to be buried, in Avila or Alba de Tormes, where she now lay. "Do I have to have anything of my own?" she asked. "Won't they give me a bit of earth here?" She died on the feast of St. Francis, October 4, 1582. So gently did she breathe forth her spirit that no one knew exactly when the moment of death came. Forty years later, the church canonized Teresa de Capeda y Ahumada, and in 1970 she was proclaimed a doctor of the universal church.

In September, 1970, Vatican authorities proclaimed St. Teresa of Avila a doctor of the universal church. She is the first woman in history to receive this honor.

Satoko Kitahara

Rising majestically from beneath the horizon's purple rim, the morning sun released a glistening stream of roseate light across the gray, chilly waters of Tokyo Bay. Sailors on watch aboard vessels rising at anchor in Yokohama Harbor squinted into the dawn. Stevedores and dock workers, ministering to huge merchant ships snuggled against long, gray piers, felt the sun's first warmth. In a shantytown section of the marshlands bordering the bay, ragpickers emerged from their packing-crate huts, picked up large, empty wicker baskets and trotted silently toward Tokyo's back alleys and refuse heaps to harvest the day's junk.

As the day began, that morning in July, 1951, the sun's rays could hardly have fallen on a sight more tender than that in the Tokyo marshes. A group of Japanese children, clad in rags and holding hands, stood in a circle around a huge, untidy pyramid of large milk cans. The children, like miniature Shinto priests worshiping around a gnarled and ancient tree, circled slowly from left to right around the metal tower. A young woman, herself part of the circle, led them in song. Tiny voices, sweet and light, rose up to greet the morning sun. "Oh, happy is the little child," they sang. The sun's rays bounced off the milk cans, imprinting little rainbows of color on the dull metal. Warm, pink light washed across the cheerful faces of the children.

These were the Ant Children, the despised offspring of Tokyo's outcasts, contemptuously called the Ant People. The homeless Ant People of Tokyo's grubby underside ranked lowest on the social scale of the Japanese people. On this July morning, the scorned and spurned children danced in the sun.

A man suddenly appeared and summoned the young woman, Satoko Kitahara, from the circle. Dressed in the ragpicker's uniform of a battered peak cap, loose gray shirt, and serge trousers tucked into black rubber knee boots, the man bowed graciously to the young lady. Ant Town's moral leader, he was called The Professor. He ruled a population of orphans, vagrants, dispossessed, panhandlers, welfare cases, black marketeers, alcoholics, and ex-jailbirds that squatted illegally in tin and cardboard huts on a site city planners had chosen for a municipal park. The Ant Towners, however, had successfully fended off every official attempt to drive them from their spongy turf.

Ant Town had its monuments, towers of debris strewn about the muddy paths and puddled streets. Piles of rusted tin cans, broken buckets, cast-off toys,

Ant Town children adored Satoko. No matter how much fatigue she experienced, she saw to it that the little ones did not escape their daily schoolwork, singing, and hot baths.

scorched sheets of galvanized iron, straw ropes, and rubber shoes decorated the landscape. Mounds of damp newspapers, cement bags, rusted oil drums, broken panes of glass, and automobile springs festooned the marsh grass. A World War II Quonset hut was Ant Town's major architectural feature. Some forty feet long, the building lay like a fat, exhausted dog in the morning sun. Its tin roof, jagged and battered, raised rusted iron teeth in defiance into the sky.

Before the hut's entrance stretched a small cement plaza that served as a town square. On the square's broken cement, children sang and danced around their milk-can tower on that morning of joy.

After Satoko and The Professor exchanged the requisite bows and appropriate small talk, The Professor inquired about the celebration occurring before him. "I told you, Professor," the young woman said, "the Lady would not let us down."

"I don't understand you, Satoko," he responded; "I don't know whether you are an angel or a devil."

atoko chats with Matsui Sensei, the Ant Town guru whose wisdom and courage won him
e title The Professor.

*   *   *   *   *

Born in Suginami, an affluent Tokyo suburb, on August 22, 1929, Satoko Kitahara never knew poverty. Her mother, Eiko, came from a wealthy family. Her father, a descendant of generations of Shinto chief priests, had earned a doctoral degree in agriculture. Since the Japanese revere their teachers as members of a sacred profession, Professor Kinji Kitahara enjoyed great prestige. He also earned a generous income from the family's shoe business.

Although the Great Depression of the 1930s created severe economic suffering in Japan, the Kitaharas maintained a comfortable home and provided a fine education for their three daughters and one son.

Satoko and her young sisters, Keiko and Etsuko, learned the demands Japanese society placed on a young lady of breeding. The three girls gave unquestioned loyalty to their Emperor, respect and obedience to their father, love and deference to their mother. They learned that, in the Japanese family, the brother came first. As proper Japanese young women, they presumed their parents

Satoko Kitahara (extreme left, kneeling) with her family in Tokyo.

would arrange their marriages and, once wedded, they would walk behind their husbands, with toes pointed inward to appear awkward. As good wives, they would never offer an opinion. If someone insisted, they would say, "I have no idea," or, "I entirely agree with my husband." They accepted it as commonplace for the Japanese husband to refer to his spouse in conversation as "my stupid wife."

A contemporary of Satoko described the severity of a young girl's training. "A girl of ten or twelve will not even lift her eyes to look at a dish of ice cream melting before her, since it would be impolite. She must be forced to draw near and eat the ice cream."

Estu Sugimoto, a Japanese authoress writing in 1926, recalled a Confucian scholar teaching her at age six to memorize the Chinese classics. "Throughout my two-hour lesson, he never moved the slightest fraction of an inch except for his hands and lips. I sat before him on the matting in an equally correct and unchanging position. Once, in the midst of a lesson, I swayed my body slightly, allowing my folded knee to slip a trifle from the proper angle. The faintest shade of surprise crossed my instructor's face. Very quietly he closed his book, saying gently but with a stern air: 'Little Miss, it is evident your mental attitude today is not suited for study. You should retire to your room and meditate.' My little heart was almost killed with shame."

When Japanese educational authorities established schools for the higher education of women, they loaded curricula heavily with instruction in etiquette and bodily movement. One president of a school for girls of upper-middle-class families arranged for his students to learn European languages so "they would be able to put their husbands' books back in the bookcase right side up after they had dusted them off."

There was another side to this picture. "A woman runs her servants, has great say in her children's marriages," a contemporary of Satoko wrote, "and, when she is a mother-in-law, commonly runs her household realm with as firm a hand as if she had never been, for half her life, a nodding violet.... The Japanese grandmother serenely expects everyone to do as she approves; there is no scolding nor arguing, but her expectations, soft as silk floss and quite as strong, hold her little family to the paths that seem right to her."

Professor Kitahara, deeply committed to the tenets of Japanese family customs, could not, in his wildest imagination, dream that his charming, graceful,

Satoko at age thirteen was growing into a charming, graceful, highly intelligent young Japanese woman.

highly intelligent little Satoko — who sat motionless before her tutors, who bowed and danced graciously when ceremony demanded, who refused to touch her food until ordered, who sat patiently while her ice cream melted — would smash the mold.

* * * * *

When war broke out between Japan and the United States in December, 1941, Professor Kitahara and his son were drafted. The father entered the armed forces, the son enlisted for factory work.

By 1944, fifteen-year-old Satoko joined the war workers at Tokyo's Nakajima aircraft factory.

Day and night, American bombers pounded Tokyo, turning the city into a sea of flames. The few remaining Japanese Zero fighters and antiaircraft guns failed to halt the carnage. More than once, Satoko almost died at her factory bench. "If I am to die," she told a fellow worker, "let me die with a friend."

Government authorities urged their people to work unceasingly despite the bombings and slaughter. Workers dropped from exhaustion. "The weaker our bodies, the stronger our spirit," boasted military officers safe in their under ground bunkers. "We must match

Japanese discipline against American numbers and Japanese flesh against American steel," they exhorted.

On August 14, 1945, one day before the emperor formally surrendered Japan, Satoko collapsed at her factory bench, a victim of tuberculosis. Her brother, not so fortunate, died of exhaustion. Since her father was still away at war, the severely ill Satoko, although near death, observed Japanese custom and acted as chief mourner at her brother's funeral.

As American administrators, merchants, educators, industrialists, and missionaries poured into the country after the war, the Japanese found themselves questioning their most hallowed traditions. American women, serving in all ranks of the military as well as in secretarial and executive capacities, at first shocked them. The Japanese were entirely unprepared for the warmth and gentleness of the American GI toward women.

Coca-Cola, jukeboxes, short skirts, lipstick, do-wop singing, and American dancing fascinated Japanese youth. In the spiritual chaos of American occupation, they found it difficult to decide whether they were Japanese or Americans. The inner turmoil and confusion of her contemporaries deeply affected the intelligent, sensitive Satoko who, by her own admission, became as silly and confused as any of her peers.

After her health improved in the fall of 1946, Satoko enrolled in Tokyo's Showa Women's Pharmaceutical College. During her student years, Satoko often slipped off to a hillside overlooking the Yokohama Harbor in Tokyo Bay. The solitude and the view of ships riding at anchor in the calm, glistening waters relaxed her. One day, while walking

While enrolled in Tokyo's Showa Women's Pharmaceutical College, Satoko often took walks on the shore overlooking Yokohama Harbor in Tokyo Bay.

with a friend along the bay, she spotted two nuns dressed in their religious habit entering a tiny church. Although neither she nor her companion was Catholic, on impulse, they followed the nuns into the church. Satoko found herself standing before a statue of the Blessed Mother. The beauty of the statue's face pierced her heart. For months afterward, she reflected on this experience. She determined to discover more about the person whom the statue represented and the nuns who had led her into that mysterious, wondrous place.

The nuns, she learned, belonged to the religious order known as Mercedarians. Members of the community had been interned during the war, but despite harsh treatment in some cases, they had nothing but love and the deepest respect for the Japanese people. She persuaded her father to enroll her younger sister in Tokyo's Mercedarian College. When Satoko visited her sister there, she met the assistant principal, Mother Angela.

Mother Angela asked Satoko if she had been baptized. "No," responded the bewildered young woman who hardly knew the meaning of the word. "Why don't you prepare yourself for baptism and become a Christian?" asked the nun. Four months after Mother Angela's invitation, Satoko was baptized and given the Christian name Elizabeth on October 30, 1949. A few days later, she was confirmed and chose Maria as her middle name. The same year, she graduated as a pharmacist.

Mother Angela belonged to the Mercedarian Missionaries, a religious institute which shared the heritage of the Mercedarians founded by St. Peter Nolasco in the thirteenth century in Spain. To the vows of poverty, chastity, and obedience, Mecedarian priests and

Mother Maria Angela de Aguirre and Satoko Kitahara on the day of Satoko's baptism.

brothers added a fourth, to offer themselves as hostages in place of Christians whom North African Moslems had taken captive and enslaved. Modeling their efforts on that of Christ, who gave his life that others might live forever, white-garbed Mercedarians freed fellow Christians by taking their places in Moslem prisons, galley benches, servant quarters, and forced labor gangs.

The impressionable young Satoko absorbed a similar exalted notion of Christian service from her inspiration, Mother Angela. Once the young Japanese girl grasped the Mercedarian ideal of offering one's freedom, even life, for another, she understood why these nuns bore their wartime internment in Japan so cheerfully.

To help Japanese converts to Catholicism appreciate the role of service of one's neighbor, Mother Angela directed a number of programs to benefit postwar Tokyo's poor. She warned her young charges that, if they chose to follow Christ in

the Mercedarian manner, suffering, perhaps even death, could ensue. Mercedarian spirituality, arching across the centuries from the bloody shores of the medieval Mediterranean to bomb-blasted twentieth-century Tokyo, shaped the Christian life of Satoko Kitahara.

*   *   *   *   *

Brother Zeno Zebrowski, O.F.M. Conv., a second major influence in Satoko's life, arrived in Japan in May, 1930, with a group of Polish Conventual Franciscans headed by Maximilian Kolbe, who established a friary in the hills above Nagasaki, the Catholic center of Japan.

Franciscan Brother Zeno Zebrowski's works of charity made him a household name in Japan from the time of his arrival in 1930. Children flocked to him wherever he went.

Ant Town citizens, dressed in uniforms that identified their humble status, swarmed into Tokyo each morning to collect and sort junk. Through hard work and shrewd bargaining, they managed to scratch out a meager living and preserve their independence and dignity.

The physically powerful, barrel-chested Zeno, in his black conventual Franciscan habit, walked down from the friary each day to the city. Standing in the town square — his face framed by a huge beard and shock of black hair, and bright with cherubic joy — he begged for Nagasaki's poor. He greeted each person who passed him in fractured Japanese. Although Nagasaki's citizens hardly understood his words, they immediately sensed his deep love and compassion for the poor. To each person he greeted, he handed a holy-card picture of the Blessed Mother. When his begging was finished, he went to the poor quarters of the city to distribute all he had received. As the years passed, he became a Nagasaki institution. When war hysteria gripped Japan, Zeno, alone of all foreign priests, sisters, and brothers, was not interned. The government allowed him to travel through the entire nation to do his works of mercy. The emperor provided him with a personal letter that urged anyone whom the Franciscan approached to support his works. In Japan, a credential of that order amounted to a direct imperial command.

Satoko met Zeno shortly after her conversion to Catholicism. The Franciscan, who had come to search out Tokyo's poor and needy, specifically sought to assist the unique community of the Ant People. She said to her father, "If foreigners can come all the way from Poland to dedicate their lives to the service of the poor in Japan, why shouldn't we Japanese Christians do the same?"

*   *   *   *   *

Following World War II and during the American occupation, Japan teetered on the edge of economic chaos. The homeless, beggars, criminals, black marketeers, prostitutes, drug pushers, and drifters swarmed into Tokyo. Some of the less desirable citizens squatted illegally in Ant Town. The city people considered Ant Towners as failures and dropouts who contributed little to the reconstruction of Japan. Tokyo's city fathers, viewing Ant Town as an eyesore and constant reminder of the consequences of military defeat, made frequent but unsuccessful efforts to wipe it out.

Ant Towners themselves rejected all charges of criminal behavior and opposed every effort to destroy their village. They rejected both crime and welfare as means for escaping poverty. Headed by Ozawa San, a convicted

The Professor (Matsui Sensei), a philosopher and cynic, The Boss (Ozawa San), an ex-con and natural leader, and Satoko, a mystic and daughter of privilege, joined forces to form as unlikely a group of apostles as ever labored in the church.

criminal called The Boss, and guru Matsui Sensei, called The Professor, the Ant Town people banded together in a community effort to survive by collecting junk and other refuse and selling it on the market. Each morning ragpickers swarmed through Tokyo streets, alleys, and bombed-out sections, scouring refuse heaps, picking through dumpsters and garbage pails, looking for salable materials. Although Ant Towners had lost everything — reputation, social standing, possibilities of reaping reward from Japan's nascent industrialism — they refused charity from others as patronizing, demeaning, and dehumanizing. They clung to their community as the only way to preserve their fierce pride. Their determination to maintain Ant Town was as strong as the city officials' determination to destroy it.

As the ongoing battle between the Ant People and city authorities reached a climax, Brother Zeno, like an old war horse smelling combat, appeared in Tokyo.

The Professor and The Boss, consistent with their disdain for outside charity, did not welcome Zeno's offer to help. Nevertheless, they gave him a hearing. In mangled Japanese, he assured them that he could rescue Ant Town. "I'll get you some favorable publicity," the friar announced.

By 1950 the Japanese, sick of war's aftermath of misery and poverty, were determined to eliminate want and all signs of suffering from their islands. In this postwar atmosphere, Zeno, once so highly esteemed, became an embarrassment. When he sought media attention in Tokyo, he discovered that impeccably polite Japanese editors were not interested in him or his cause.

In the face of this disappointment, The Professor, a wily strategist, devised a bold plan. Capitalizing on postwar interest in Western religion and knowing how Roman Catholicism particularly excited Japanese curiosity, he phoned a number of newspaper editors. "Brother Zeno is in Ant Town," he announced. "We are planning to build a church here." To insure an immediate response, The Professor added: "Brother Zeno is here for only a few moments. He plans on leaving now. I will hold him here only if you wish." The ruse worked. A TV team showed up immediately in Ant Town.

Just before the team arrived, The Professor told Zeno of his rash promise. "Never mind," said the irrepressible Franciscan, "Ant Town will have a church." Brother Zeno left The Professor, walked out to the Quonset hut's broken concrete plaza, knelt down and began to say the rosary. The TV crew appeared and wasted no time in filming the Franciscan brother at prayer. That night, the old man, kneeling in his habit amid Ant Town rubble and praying the rosary, appeared on TV screens all over Japan.

Satoko, while scanning a newspaper the following day, saw a picture of Zeno at prayer in Ant Town and read that he, whom she had met casually some months earlier, had dedicated himself to help its residents build their own church.

On a cold, damp winter night in early December, 1950, Satoko arrived in Ant Town and introduced herself to Zeno. The Professor and The Boss, regarding her as just another patronizing wealthy do-gooder, were not impressed. Zeno, however, received her kindly and, after a short visit, offered to accompany her back to her home. As they walked through Tokyo, he pointed out the homeless, ex-soldiers, the poor, vagrants, prostitutes, war orphans — sleeping on sidewalks, clustered around campfires in public parks, huddled in public toilets. He led the sheltered, highly cultured young woman on a tour through a chamber of horrors. She soon realized the friar cared deeply for these outcasts. While her own countrymen attempted to believe these unfortunates did not exist, he made their pain his own.

Initially, Satoko lived a double life between her beautiful and aristocratic family home and the ramshackle buildings of Ant Town, until The Professor challenged her to give her life for her Christ by living among the people of Ant Town.

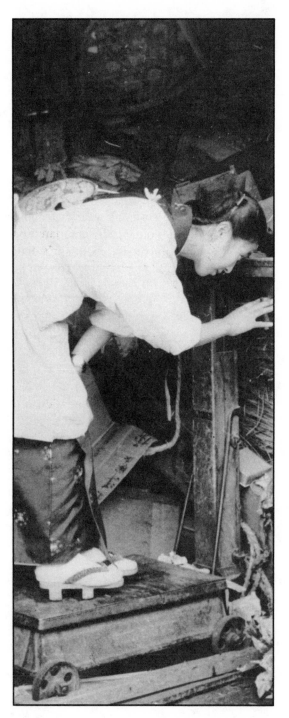

After they arrived at Satoko's home, Zeno produced from his briefcase a series of photographs of poor people throughout Japan. As he displayed these pictures, he spoke with deepest sympathy of the unfortunate, the lonely, the war-wracked, the crippled and homeless. Satoko served him hot tea and sandwiches, but the enthused Zeno scarcely ate. After supper, he bade her good night and returned to Ant Town through the cold, wet night.

Satoko did not sleep that night. Zeno's words kept running through her mind. Most of all, the old man's face, shining with kindness, compassion, and determination to serve the poor, filled her mind. The fact that he had left his own home so many years ago and dedicated himself to her people challenged the young woman. She compared her life to his. She was twenty-one years old, a respected university professor's daughter, well-off. Neighbors called her beautiful home The Flower Manor. Beneficiary of a fine education, she could speak a few

foreign languages, play the piano, while away hours at motion pictures, musical concerts, or silly amusements.

By morning, she resolved to serve the poor, regardless of the cost. "How utterly blind I have been," she whispered into the new day. "I am ashamed."

A few days after leading Satoko through nighttime Tokyo, Zeno asked her to organize a Christmas celebration in Ant Town. Arriving at the place, she encountered signs that the town's citizens had already begun preparations. The ragpickers had festooned the gates of the town with silver and gold tinsel scrounged from Tokyo department stores. A ten-foot-tall Santa Claus stood beside the entrance gate. Satoko quickly mobilized the children. She discovered they knew nothing about Christ, except

Ant Towners gathered at the village gate for a community celebration.

that he was a Western world hero and born poor. They had created their decorations and set up their Santa Claus simply to imitate Western customs.

She also discovered that the ragged children could not, in the few days left them, learn the Western Christmas carols she had planned to teach them. She settled for a couple of Japanese children's songs. In thin, piping voices, the little ones, who had never seen anything but Tokyo streets, sang "Cedar Saplings Growing on the Mountain Top." Satoko added "Sunset" and "Dragonfly" to their Christmas concert repertoire.

Following the song rehearsal, the children sat in a circle around Satoko. Starved for affection, they opened their hearts to the lovely young woman who taught them how to sing. From innocent children came stories of drunken fathers, broken homes, and bitterness at the rejection they experienced from other children. "They shout at us and insult us," one little tot wept, "as if we have no feelings." Satoko could hardly restrain her tears. To have heard these stories from Brother Zeno disturbed her mind. Hearing them from little children themselves broke her heart. "I'll be your big sister," she told them. "I'll be on your side and I'll fight for you!"

On Christmas Eve, 1950, in the full glare of television lights, the celebration began in Ant Town. The event, a Christmas celebration in a ghetto, was too good for the media, whom Brother Zeno had alerted, to miss. Twenty or thirty ragpickers as shepherds, The Boss' goat as a sheep, The Boss himself playing chief shepherd, little children dressed up like shining stars — all moved in colorful procession toward a small straw hut where a real baby slept on a bed of straw. The Boss' wife, wearing a white veil on her head, played Mary. Satoko had managed to teach the children one Latin hymn, *Gloria in Excelsis Deo*. They sang the ancient prayer with great reverence. As ceremonies concluded, Zeno dropped to his knees before the straw hut and began praying the rosary. As TV cameras swept across Ant Town, its residents, one by one, fell to their knees.

The Professor knelt beside Zeno. As Zeno finished his prayers, he murmured to The Professor, "Thank you, thank you."

"Don't thank me," the crusty Ant Town leader responded; "Satoko made all this preparation."

After the procession, Ant Town residents gathered to feast at a table piled high with squid and oranges. Newspaper reporters and TV cameramen, delighted

During Ant Town's Christmas Eve celebration, Japanese TV featured The Boss, Brother Zeno, and Satoko praying the rosary at the conclusion of the festival.

with their story, departed. Soon after the feast began, the electricity went off. Satoko, surrounded by little ones, told ghost stories until her listeners' heads nodded and, one by one, they slipped into the darkness to the tiny tin and cardboard hovels they called home.

*   *   *   *   *

The Professor, although admiring Satoko's dedication to the children, still distrusted her. "You do not live for us, Satoko, but only for your Christ. You love him — not us," he charged. Further, he frequently chided her that she did not understand the Ant Town people. "We are proud of our ability to live off junk." Again and again, he said to her: "We would rather starve than accept charity. We will live in meanest poverty rather than accept food and shelter we have not earned." Ant Towners — tough, independent, and outwardly grubby — did not understand Satoko. She seemed naive to them. The Professor found it impossible to consider the cultured young woman as one of them or to believe she loved them.

To complicate matters, The Professor distrusted Christians. A crafty, hard-nosed survivor and member of the Eta, Japan's poorest class, he had lost respect early in life for the rigid establishment controlling the destinies of the Japanese people. He relished his role as shepherd of a despised flock. Thumbing his nose at everything and everybody respectable, he spurned gestures of help from anyone outside the Ant Town community.

Satoko's simplicity, naivete, and cheerfulness, as well as her obvious love for the Ant Town children and their joy in her presence, finally convinced him that, although the young woman would never understand the Ant People, she was at least trying.

One particular effort proved her sincerity. From someone in Ant Town she obtained a ragpicker's large wicker basket. Within an hour of her first day of ragpicking, she collected a basketful of straw rope and loose straw that she

Satoko cheerfully accepted the rag-picker's basket as a badge of her citizenship in Ant Town.

sold for a hundred yen. The Professor, to show his pleasure, presented her with an Ant Town junk cart for her own use. That gesture advanced her in the town's estimation.

The next morning, pulling her junk cart through the streets of Tokyo, Satoko felt herself more and more like an Ant Towner. Ordinary Japanese who encountered the beautiful young woman of obvious breeding pulling a junk cart assumed she had gone mad. "Probably a war casualty," they thought.

Each day after finishing her ragpicking and junk-sorting, she instructed the children in basic grammar as well as singing, music, and dancing. After classes she supervised the children's afternoon baths. From two to four o'clock, a towel in one hand and a bar of soap in the other, she washed their backs. She made sure that the children disinfected their washcloths with creosol solution before bathing in an oil drum filled with hot water.

Despite all her love, all the affection exchanged between herself and the children, and all her services, The Professor still regarded her as the little rich girl playing Lady Bountiful. She lived with her parents and returned to her posh suburban home each night after her work. Upon her return home, her mother stripped Satoko of her kimono, took it outside, shook gnats from it, and then hurled her underclothes into a tub of boiling water. Although Satoko was breaking every rule for young women of her class and station, her mother and father never interfered or resented what others of their status termed eccentric behavior.

Shortly after Christmas, 1950, The Professor and The Boss decided to build an Ant Town center, a two-story building that would contain a meeting room, school, and bathhouse. After gathering boards, wires, bricks, nails, cement, and glass from Tokyo's junk heaps, the Ant Towners quickly erected their building. The Professor, of course, ignored such legal niceties as building permits, variances, and other regulations. Shortly after completion of the center, the city fathers declared the building illegal and threatened to demolish it.

At Nagasaki, Brother Zeno got word of the condemnation and sped to Tokyo. After consulting The Professor, he visited municipal authorities. "You cannot bulldoze that building," he muttered through his great beard. "As you heard last year, we are going to build a church at Ant Town."

"Wait until the end of May for your church," the city fathers countered. "We plan a children's exhibition in the park next to Ant Town and we do not want any construction going on." In reality, authorities had already decided to destroy Ant Town before the end of May.

"Please, sirs," Zeno responded, "will you be good enough to put your decision on paper so that, when I get home, I can read it and understand. My knowledge of Japanese is so limited I must study your words." To accommodate the friar, the city clerk wrote: "If the church is to be built, it cannot be constructed before May 1 of next year."

Zeno returned to Ant Town, gave the note to The Professor and left for Nagasaki.

On Friday of the second week of May, 1951, engineers ordered the demolition of the Ant Town center. City fathers went even further with orders for the demolition of the entire shantytown. Work was scheduled to start on the morning of May 14.

With only two days' grace, The Professor held an emergency meeting. "They are going to bulldoze us Monday morning," he told The Boss. Then The Professor recalled the city clerk's note to Zeno. "That note granted us permission to build a church after May 1, 1951, he said. "If we can have a church here on Monday morning, they won't dare bulldoze us."

The two men sat in silence. Then The Professor said, "How can we build a church in two days?"

The Boss, who owed his survival to his wits, responded, "That's easy." Summoning an Ant Town resident, a skillful carpenter, he ordered him to immediately construct a six-foot tall wooden

The simple cross rising above the Ant Town center, fulfilling Brother Zeno's promise to build a church, saved the squatters' village from bulldozers of the Tokyo municipality.

cross which he and The Professor raised atop the roof of the center on May 13, Pentecost Sunday. Ant Town had its church! When the engineers appeared Monday morning, The Professor waved the city clerk's letter in their faces and pointed to the cross. The bulldozers withdrew.

*   *   *   *   *

During the summer following the raising of the cross on the Ant Town center, Satoko planned an excursion for the children to the Hakone mountain resort near the outskirts of Tokyo. Assuring The Professor that there was no charity involved, she told him a friend of hers had offered the use of his summer cottage for four days in August. The Professor, suspecting that Satoko would use her family money for the project, demanded to know how she planned to obtain funds to pay for the children's transportation. "I don't know yet," she replied, "but God will provide for his children." The Professor said: "God better provide five to six thousand yen."

Satoko bombarded the Blessed Mother with prayers. "No one deserves a few days in the mountains more than these poor little ones," she reminded Mary.

Several nights before the planned excursion, Satoko's prayers at her tiny Marian shrine were interrupted by her mother who surprised her with good news. "Your father just phoned," she said. "A friend of his has a large quantity of empty milk cans he wants to get rid of. Would Ant Town be interested?"

"When does he want them removed?" Satoko asked.

Satoko mobilized a fleet of Ant Town's junk carts to retrieve the pile of milk cans that financed the children's trip to the mountains.

"Tonight."

Satoko rushed to Ant Town, mobilized a fleet of pull carts and led them to the treasure-trove. By dawn, a mountain of empty milk cans had risen in the Ant Town plaza and the children danced around it. The Professor's quick computation assured her that on the day's market the cans would sell for between six to seven thousand yen. She smiled and bowed, her face shining, her eyes dancing.

"Who are you, Satoko?" The Professor mused. "Who sent you?"

*   *   *   *   *

Sometime in 1950, before her first encounter with Brother Zeno, Satoka had taken an apartment in Asakusa, a Tokyo neighborhood near Ant Town. She attended daily Mass at a nearby church and, after beginning work at Ant Town, brought the children and many of their parents for Sunday Mass.

After the Ant Town center was completed, she set up study rooms in the new building. Her days, beginning with early morning ragpicking and ending with classes and other chores at night, consumed her limited energies. The pervading dampness at Ant Town, plus her exhausting pace, wore down Satoko's already frail health. The Professor watched with dismay as she poured out her energies and health on the people of Ant Town.

Her efforts attracted the attention of newspapers, magazines, TV, and radio broadcasters. The media focused

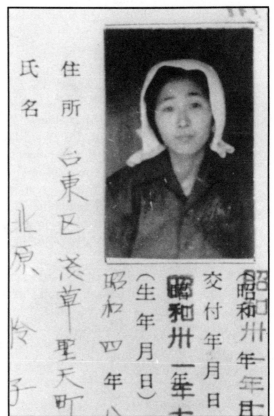

Satoko's license to collect junk in Tokyo gives official approbation to her chosen vocation. Tokyo newspapers frequently pictured her in her Ant Town outfit, although many of Tokyo's citizens assumed the obviously aristocratic young woman was a mentally unbalanced war casualty.

upon the wealthy young girl who gave herself so generously to the outcasts of Tokyo. Pictures of Satoko pushing her junk cart appeared frequently. The press referred to her as "The Mary of Ant Town." In Japanese usage the words "The Mary" referred to the Blessed Mother. She received letters from all over the country. A group of Japanese prisoners awaiting execution in the Philippines wrote to her, asking her prayers. She arranged a public Mass for their release and wrote to military authorities to seek their pardon.

Eventually, Satoko's health failed. She had to remain at home in bed. Visiting her, The Professor found her depressed. "I cannot be sleeping here at home in these warm surroundings when so many people believe I have given myself to the poor," she told him. "I am no true ragpicker. I am only a part-time butterfly who finds joy in working. I have nothing. I take all."

"Satoko," The Professor said, "I always believed you only served us because Christ demanded it; I cannot believe you truly love us. Would you," he challenged, "give your life for the people of Ant Town?"

"Yes, I would."

"Why?" The Professor asked.

"Because Christ gave his life for me. And, if he wishes me to give my life for Ant Town, I would do so." Her answer rose out of her Mercedarian spirituality.

"How do you plan to give your life for us, Satoko?" The Professor queried.

"I want to live in Ant Town. I want to leave my father and mother's home and share the life of the Ant People. I want to work and suffer with them, to rejoice with them as one of them."

"Satoko," The Professor responded, "for the first time, I believe you really love us. But, please do not come with us. You are weak, your health is poor, and you will die. You will be of no use to anyone dead." He convinced her to rest. "If you are willing to give your life for us, you'd better have a life to give," he counseled.

Satoko explained that she planned to rest and recuperate in the mountains until her health returned. With his blessing, she journeyed to the hot-springs resort in the Hakone region and remained there for almost a year. Her health gradually improved during these restful months.

Near the end of her year of recuperation, Satoko, hearing rumors that city authorities planned a final offensive against Ant Town, told her father that she planned to return to the village permanently. Worried about her health, her father asked her to remain a bit longer at the hot-springs resort. "No, father," she said. "I must return now."

She returned to Ant Town immediately. She discovered that The Boss had hired a married couple to educate the children and supervise their baths. Many children she had trained had left Ant Town; the new children did not know her. The place, she judged, functioned very well without her. She had abandoned all the luxuries her life of wealth afforded, her parents, her home, and her health, only to discover how quickly she could be replaced. The knowledge crushed her.

Of all people, The Boss, ex-felon and convicted criminal, helped her to put her life in perspective. "You told The Professor once, Satoko, that you would be willing to die for Ant Town if your Christ wanted you to do that," he said. "Don't you see the role of 'The Mary of Ant Town' was only loaned to you and now your Christ wants it back? If Christ wants it back, why don't you give it to him?" The Boss added that God was requiring everything of her, even her own will.

She bowed her head and acknowledged The Boss' wisdom. "The new couple you have hired here can do all that I can do, and perhaps do it better," she responded. "I will leave Ant Town and not return unless God calls me."

That night, The Boss called a meeting of the Ant Town Council. "We've got to let her go," he said. "The only thing I said that made sense to her was that her God, whom she claims is the most important person in her life, required this of her. I've got to tell the Council that, if that God inspired Satoko to help us, I want to have that God for my God too." His words ignited a lengthy discussion. In the end, everyone agreed that he should seek baptism.

After this decision, The Professor and all the elders decided they would like to be baptized too. The Boss took the name Zeno; The Professor, Joseph. The Professor explained his choice of name in this way: "From what I know, Joseph protected Mary. I plan to protect our Mary."

Satoko left Ant Town and returned to her home in Suginami. With Mother Angela's approval, she decided to join the Mercedarian Sisters. The morning of her departure for the convent, a high fever felled her. Her parents sent her to the hospital. Doctors placed her on the critical list. After some days, a doctor summoned her parents as well as The Boss and The Professor.

Satoko spent hours at prayer. She found strength and consolation for her hard life in daily Mass and communion.

"I can do nothing for Satoko," he told them. "There's only one hospital that can possibly help her."

"Where is this hospital?" The Boss demanded.

"Ant Town," the doctor said.

"Take her there. She might die at Ant Town. She'll probably die here. If she dies at Ant Town, she'll die happy."

After obtaining her parents' consent, The Boss brought Satoko back.

The Boss and The Professor arranged a special room for Satoko in the Ant Town center. Brother Zeno came from Nagasaki with a three-foot-tall statue of Our Lady of Lourdes. The Boss and The Professor placed the statue atop a platform directly in front of Satoko's room.

During the 1954 Marian Year, Ant Towners gathered on August 29 to celebrate a special Mass of dedication for the statue of Our Lady of Lourdes. For the first time, Mass was celebrated in the junkyard ghetto. The Chief Justice of the Supreme Court and the Chairman of the Japanese Chamber of Commerce, who later became the nation's Foreign Minister, both sent congratulatory messages.

Just as the doctor guessed, Satoko's health improved.

*   *   *   *   *

Tokyo authorities continued their relentless efforts to level Ant Town and develop a municipal park in the area. Ant Towners, with the considerable sympathy and support of city residents and the media, successfully thwarted every bureaucratic maneuver and legal stratagem. In 1957, faced with the need to provide a larger dumping ground for garbage, city fathers began reclaiming a vast tract of land from Tokyo Bay. They offered a sizable portion of the new land to Ant Towners for twenty-five million yen, cash.

The city fathers, realizing that Ant Towners, unlike other citizens, were accustomed to junk, garbage, and incinerator smoke, felt the squatters would jump at their offer. But, The Professor glumly advised Satoko, "We do not

This photo, taken during the last year of Satoko's life, clearly depicts the heavy toll of her seven years of dedicated work at Ant Town.

have twenty-five million in cash. If they would allow us to pay installments over ten years, we might make it."

"We must pray day and night to the Blessed Mother," Satoko told The Professor. To help herself pray, she tacked a large sign on her wall reading, "twenty-five million yen."

The city fathers summoned The Professor to negotiate the sale. Although he felt his efforts were doomed, the leader agreed to meet with them.

Before he left for the meeting, Satoko gave him her rosary. "It is my most precious possession, Professor," she told him; "it has been blessed by the Holy Father." She pressed it into his hand. "Go to the meeting with confidence," she added. "I will spend my day before the statue of Our Lady of Lourdes, praying the rosary. Remember, Professor, long ago I promised my Lord that I would lay down my life for Ant Town. That moment has come."

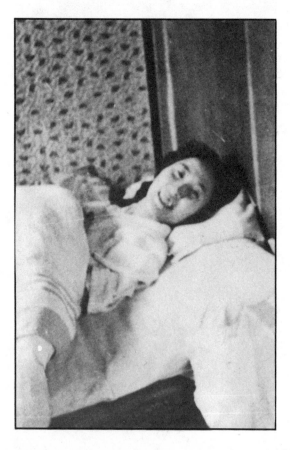

During negotiations, The Professor told the city director that the Ant Town people only wanted a place to live and continue to work. He handed the official a copy of a book Satoko had written some four years previously, called *The Children of Ant Town*. Then he held out the rosary Satoko had given him. Pointing to the cross, he said that, because of the example of Satoko who followed the example of Christ, he was willing to offer his life for others, particularly the Ant Town people. "Satoko, the young lady who wrote that book," he continued, "has also offered her life for our people. At Ant Town, we are a community of love. That makes us different."

The director, a kindly man, visited The Professor at Ant Town a few days

Tuberculosis finally confined Satoko to her bed in 1957. She died on January 23, 1958, at the age of twenty-eight.

later. During their conversation, he heard an organ resounding from the Ant Town center. "That's Satoko," The Professor said. "She is the one who has offered her life for Ant Town."

"I think I understand," responded the official. "I may be an efficient official, but I also want to be a good man."

During the weeks following the official's visit, Satoko's health steadily deteriorated, and she was once more confined to bed. When her mother asked her if there was anything she wanted, she responded: "I am so happy to be here among my friends at Ant Town, to eat their food, to share their life." She prayed her rosary constantly for the resolution of Ant Town's property problem.

On January 9, 1958, city authorities summoned The Professor. Before leaving for the meeting, he stopped at Satoko's room. Feeble though she was, she raised her thin hand, grasping her rosary, and waved to The Professor. She took the rosary's crucifix and pressed it to her lips. Too weak to speak, she nevertheless signaled The Professor that she was praying for him.

When The Professor arrived at the city office, he found a copy of *The Children of Ant Town* on the desk of the director.

"After careful study," the director told him, "the city fathers have decided to provide Ant Town land for fifteen million yen, payable in five years." That sum, the Ant Town people could easily handle.

On January 20, 1958, the new Ant Town was born. Three days later, at ten minutes before eight on the morning of January 23, Satoko Kitahara, "The Mary of Ant Town," went to her eternal rest.

She never saw the new Ant Town for which she had offered her life.

In Tama Cemetary on the outskirts of Tokyo, a woman kneels before Satoko's grave. Her final resting place has become a shrine for Japanese who escape the mad rush of the city to pray and remember at this peaceful site.